A COOK'S CALENDAR

Frances Bissell, winner of the *Observer*/Mouton Cadet Dinner Party Competition in 1983, has been called one of the best private cooks in Britain. She writes for the *Sunday Times Magazine* and *A la Carte* and has written for *Harper's & Queen*. She lives in London and works for the British Council.

A COOK'S CALENDAR
Seasonal Menus by Frances Bissell

With an introduction by Jane Grigson

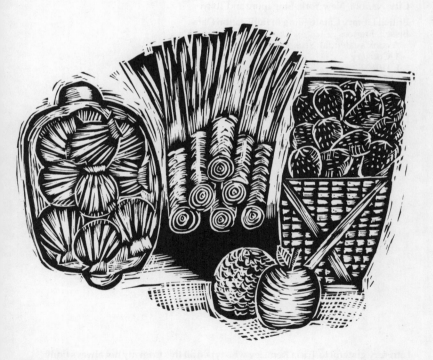

PAPERMAC

First published 1985 by Chatto & Windus, The Hogarth Press

First published in paperback 1986 by
PAPERMAC
a division of Macmillan Publishers Limited
4 Little Essex Street London WC2R 3LF

Associated companies in Auckland, Delhi, Dublin, Gaborone, Hamburg, Harare, Hong Kong, Johannesburg, Kuala Lumpur, Lagos, Manzini, Melbourne, Mexico City, Nairobi, New York, Singapore and Tokyo

British Library Cataloguing in Publication Data
Bissell, Frances
  A cook's calendar: seasonal menus.
  1. Cookery
  I. Title
  641.5'64   TX717

  ISBN 0-333-42289-9

Printed in Hong Kong

I am very grateful to Tricia Kemsley who typed all this from my not always tidily written manuscript.

CONTENTS

FOR TOM

PUBLISHER'S NOTE

Imperial and metric measurements are given in these recipes. The metric equivalents vary somewhat; for instance, in some recipes 30 g is given as an approximate equivalent for 1 oz, while in others 25 g is preferred. This is a matter of taste.

It should be remembered that the American pint is 16 fl oz in comparison to the Imperial pint, used in both Britain and Australia, which is 20 fl oz. The British standard tablespoon which has been used in this book holds 17.7 ml, the American 14.2 ml, and the Australian 20 ml. A teaspoon holds approximately 5 ml in all three countries.

INTRODUCTION

Every year the Observer Magazine holds a competition for the best dinner menu to accompany Mouton Cadet wines. When the entries came through for 1983, the judges – Victor Ceserani, Paul Levy and I – quickly recognised that one in particular, from a Mrs Frances Bissell, was a likely winner. And indeed Mrs Bissell turned out to be a star. Her dishes were simple, elegant with original touches. She cooked with good-humoured confidence. Her food tasted even better than we had anticipated.

During the stages of the competition, we discovered that Frances Bissell had kept food diaries, and her recipes, for ten years. I suggested to Jeremy Lewis at Chatto & Windus that they should ask her to write a book for them, and was delighted when the *Sunday Times* commissioned a series of articles, then a second series.

Now the book is here, as appetising as we had hoped. It exemplifies the way that our new enthusiasm for food could take us in Britain. For the last thirty-five years, since Elizabeth David published *Mediterranean Cooking* in 1950, we have opened our kitchens – not always wisely – to many new influences. In her book, Frances Bissell shows how they can be quietly absorbed into a new compatibility. She has made a web of old and new, simplifying without loss of quality. She uses seasonal ingredients and imports, for which we should be more grateful than we sometimes are, to make fresh dishes of real food. Her style is new, but she avoids the falsity of trying to imitate restaurant ways at home (anyone who has tried to organise dinner for eight with plate service at each course will understand what I mean).

Frances Bissell has a warm and approachable manner combined with high standards. Her originality and genial sense of enjoyment are evident in the way she sets one dish beside another in the various menus. She deploys familiar ingredients in unfamiliar ways, ways that are lively without being quirky or pretentious. She poaches figs in jasmin or green tea with cardamom and honey, tops a ratatouille with a cheese crumble mixture to make the main course for a vegetarian meal, makes a risotto with globe artichokes and a gratin with

Jerusalem artichokes. She has picked up an idea for tortellini stuffed with pumpkin in Italy, and sets quail eggs in a pasta nest with wild mushroom sauce. She gives her own lighter versions of fish chowder, aubergine purée, cassoulet, and introduces new favourites such as samphire. This is food that we should all like to eat, and that many of us may reasonably hope to cook.

JANE GRIGSON, 1985

PREFACE

For the last ten years I have kept a record, in diary form, of all the meals I have cooked and all the wines we have served. I use the French housewife's *agenda* for it, which gives one page a day, columns for receipts and expenditure, a recipe, and the name of the saint of the day. The front of the book contains many useful telephone numbers (useful, that is, if you live in Paris), the *legal and movable feasts*, first aid hints, how to buy and keep cosmetics, recipes for the removal of stains (fine if you know that *cambouis* is dirty grease) and a chart of temperatures for washing and ironing textiles.

The buying of these books has in itself become something of a ritual and my husband and I make a special trip to France in November to buy the *agenda*. All the big department stores have their own version of it. Once or twice we have not been able to get to France at the right time so I have had to content myself with either a desk diary or a cash book which has roughly the same format. It is now possible to buy similar diaries in Britain.

I have become very attached to my food books. The reaction of friends is rather interesting and tells me a lot about them. Those as passionately interested in food as we are think it is wonderful and why hadn't they thought of it. Others can't understand why I waste my time and think it is rather strange. A doctor friend of ours went so far as to express concern at my obsessiveness.

I don't regard it as an obsession. Food is a joy, a pleasure to be shared. It is an expression of yourself. For me it is the one area in which I have time and energy to be creative. At the end of a week of brainwork there is nothing more enjoyable than planning, shopping for and preparing meals whether it is for the two of us or for friends. Not just at weekends, for as I have mentioned already, I record all the meals I have cooked. I cook a meal every night for my husband and myself; it may be simple, perhaps a soup or a pâté followed by a pot roast French chicken with green salad, some cheese or fruit, or – more elaborate – a *salade composée* followed by a seafood lasagne using home-made pasta. But it will always be carefully planned and prepared, good to eat and worth spending time over with a shared bottle of wine.

When I think about food, I find I tend automatically to see each item in relation to others, to think in menus rather than single dishes. And that is what I am concentrating on here, in this book. My sort of cooking does not require expensive ingredients. I always try to use what is in season because it is always fresher and better value. If one of my recipes requires only part of the whole, for example, duck breasts, I suggest ways of using the rest of the duck and so you will not feel, as I do not, that you are being extravagant.

Seasonal, yes. But seasons vary throughout even a small island like ours. Summer vegetables will be available in the south of England several weeks earlier than in Scotland. And availability varies, too, which I try to keep in mind. The area of North London in which I live provides every kind of food item imaginable, and at all times of the year. My parents used to live near a small town in Derbyshire where it is sometimes difficult to buy things we take for granted in the South East – aubergines and artichokes for example. Remembering this, wherever possible I give alternative ingredients. Not everyone can find sorrel for their *noisettes* of lamb with sorrel sauce, but watercress makes an admirable alternative. It will taste different and gives the dish a different name but is equally delicious. Only once do I remember eating something really out of season. In a restaurant one cold, snowy January night I was tempted by the sight of rich, glossy, fresh strawberries on the sweet trolley. They were from Mexico and very expensive. I'm sure they would have tasted delicious in Mexico. Here they tasted of nothing, had little fragrance and I simply felt guilty. Why hadn't I ordered a slice of freshly baked apple tart made with good, crisp English Russets? I should have waited until the strawberry season, for English strawberries in June. After having eaten my fill of strawberries and cream, I could have made strawberry conserve to eat with buttermilk scones and clotted cream, strawberry shortcake, strawberry sorbet, strawberry sauce for *coeur à la crème*. There's nothing like a good old-fashioned surfeit to satisfy you until the next season.

Serving and presentation have become an important part of my cooking so I refer to the sort of plates and dishes I use. Where appropriate (and I find it usually is) I add a comment or two about the wine or wines we serve with a particular meal, or in the case of the white chocolate mousse, do not serve.

Much has already been written about the importance of getting to know the men and women who supply your raw materials. I can only underline that. The supplier I know best is my fishmonger because we tend to eat more fish, game and poultry than red meat, but if beef, lamb and pork were what we liked best I should certainly get to know my butcher. My greatest difficulty is with fruit and vegetables. Our greengrocers, both in shops and markets, still seem to object if you try to select your own produce. I have now more or less admitted defeat and go to a large supermarket which has an excellent array of varied fruit and vegetables, all in perfect condition, which I select myself. It upsets me sometimes to think that I shall be partly responsible for putting small shopkeepers out of business but I can't help thinking that they are also to blame.

I have called this book *A Cook's Calendar* for it represents three essential aspects of my food books and my cooking alike – the practical, the seasonal and, above all, the personal. It is not intended to represent a particular way of life, of eating, of entertainment. Influences and inspiration have come from many sources; from the great modern cookery writers, Elizabeth David and Jane Grigson; from travels in Italy, France and America; from the good example set by my parents, Robert Maloney who makes the best English breakfast in the world and Mary who bakes like a dream and whose Yorkshire pudding I would never try to emulate; from our fishmonger Mr T. Foster who has taught us all we know about fish; from the restaurants we have eaten in and, particularly, from those cooks and chefs who have had time to discuss their cooking; from Paul Levy and Claudia Roden who, together with Jane Grigson, have shown me great kindness and provided the encouragement, support and good advice which has helped me so much; from my husband Tom above all who is the most gifted shopper I know – how would I have learned what to do with scabbard fish and baby kid had he not brought them home from shopping trips? All these have been important in my development as a cook. As have all the countless friends who have eaten with us and who, without knowing it, provide much of the material for this book. All of them have my gratitude. Tom has most.

AUTUMN

For me the year very definitely begins in autumn. This is partly because our daily life runs according to the academic year, partly because, however long ago you were at school, the rhythm of the year seems to provide for a natural starting point in autumn, and this stays with us. January 1st is a very arbitrary starting point, the middle of winter, the middle of the school year, half-way between holidays, not the start of anything at all.

But the change from summer to autumn is noticeable; holidays are over, new theatre productions open, summer clothes are put away. The game season opens and we are back to months with an R in them so we can start buying shellfish again. From a cook's point of view therefore, autumn is very definitely a beginning again.

As evenings darken, the idea of spending a few hours in a warm kitchen is pleasant to contemplate. So this is a time to entertain friends and family to long leisurely meals. And what will you give them? Game, certainly. Not in huge quantities. One grouse between two is quite sufficient. But pigeons are delicious and, at the time of writing, a mere tenth of the price of grouse. And game is so versatile: casseroles, sauces for pasta, soups, pies, salads and puddings as well as the more glamorous *noisettes* of venison, breast of wild duck and *salmis* of pheasant.

Shellfish and particularly mussels have always been a treat for me. I first tasted mussels in a school in south-western France where I spent a year as an *assistante*. The chef was paid more than the principal and guarded his secrets well but tactfully, for he would always let me watch in the kitchen, but would never discuss. For a hundred pupils and a handful of staff he would turn out the most marvellous meals. On my first day there in mid-October 1968, tired from an overnight journey, feeling rather lost, lonely and uncertain of my French, I was taken into the bare, tiled, old-fashioned dining room, given my own heavy, red and green checked napkin, seated in front of a steaming plate of delicious *blanquette de veau* followed by a chunk of mature Cantal and a juicy, ripe William pear. Rough bread and rougher wine were to hand. I was allowed to sleep in the afternoon. By the time I sat down for supper I was beginning to realise my good fortune, knowing I was going to live in this wonderful place for a whole year. Supper was the largest tureen of the most delicious *moules marinière* I have ever tasted.

Finish now with the juicy peaches and nectarines. You will often see them in the shops into October but they will generally have come out of a freezer or cold store. Turn instead to the luscious golden Muscat grapes from Italy, the most fragrant, grapey variety you can find. Choose too the first of the English apples; first the Discovery and the Worcester Pearmain, then the Charles Ross, the Russet and the Cox's Orange Pippin. There are, of course, many more varieties of apples grown here, but we rarely see them. They are expensive to produce, therefore not cheap to buy. Not nearly as cheap as the French Golden Delicious which fill so many supermarket and green-grocers' shelves. And to go with your good, crisp apples, look out for some of the cheeses made from summer milk which are now coming to maturity. As well as the delicious English farmhouse cheeses, now is the time to look for unpasteurised Brie and Camembert, for the firm Cantal from the Auvergne and the soft, melting Vacherin.

STUFFED VINE LEAVES
GRAVAD LAX
QUAILS WITH APPLES
CARAMEL CREAM

This is very much an end of summer meal, the vine leaves are large and shiny, perfect for stuffing; any later and they begin to go leathery and change colour. The last of the salmon is in the shops at the end of August, early September. You've been eating it poached or grilled all summer, so here is another method which is particularly suited to the large fillets available at this time of year.

As for the quails, I like to think of them having fattened up on the stubble fields at the end of the harvest. Even if they didn't, small though they are, they make a surprisingly tasty and satisfying morsel. I find one per serving quite enough, but you may like to serve a couple each.

With the *gravad lax* I might serve a chilled vodka, schnapps or kümmel or if I wanted to stick to wine, a Blanquette de Limoux, a fresh, dry, sparkling wine which is still cheaper than the cheapest non-vintage champagne and better than some of them in my view. A good Rhône wine would be excellent with the quails, a Côte Rôtie if you can afford it, of a respectable vintage, or a Châteauneuf-du-Pape or Saint-Joseph from a good shipper such as Jaboulet.

Stuffed vine leaves
MAKES 24

These are good to have around for snacks so I usually make a double portion. If you can't get fresh vine leaves, vacuum-packed ones from Cyprus are very good once you've washed the brine off them. Swiss chard or spinach could be stuffed in the same way, as could firm lettuce leaves. The ingredients for the stuffing can be varied. You may already have some cooked pork or chicken, or you may choose to use dried apricots instead of raisins.

2 dozen vine leaves
8 oz / 225 g cooked rice
6 oz / 175 g cooked minced lamb
Fresh mint leaves, chopped

Pinenuts or chopped walnuts
Raisins
Crushed garlic
2 tablespoons olive oil

Wash and blanch the vine leaves. I do this by putting them in a wire sieve or colander and pouring boiling water over them. Mix all the other ingredients together, except the oil. Put a spoonful of the mixture on to the underside of a vine leaf, roll up, tucking in the ends and place, loose end down, in an earthenware dish. Continue until all the leaves and mixture are used up. If you pack the rolls tightly enough, they will not unwrap. Sprinkle the oil over and bake in the oven at gas mark 4, 180°C / 350°F, for 15 minutes. These are best served warm or cold, not piping hot.

Gravad lax
SERVES 4–6

A traditional Scandinavian dish, whose name means buried salmon, this has become a popular starter.

1½ lbs / 700 g salmon, tailpiece or middle cut
2 tablespoons fresh dill or 1 of dill seed

1 tablespoon sea salt
1 teaspoon black pepper
1 teaspoon sugar
1 tablespoon brandy

Ask your fishmonger to fillet the fish into two pieces, removing the skin.

Mix the dill, salt, pepper, sugar and brandy together. Spread the skin side of one fillet with a third of the pickle and place it, pickle side down, in a china or earthenware dish. Spread a third of the mixture on top of the fillet and place the other piece of fish on top. Finally spread it with the remaining mixture. Cover with foil or clingfilm and weight it down with tins. Leave for at least 12 hours. I find it is at its most perfect between two and three days old.

To serve, slice as smoked salmon or in vertical slices. A sweetish mustardy mayonnaise usually accompanies this which you make by adding a scant teaspoonful of sugar and a tablespoon of mustard to a basic mayonnaise. Summer sauce (p. 129) makes a nice alternative.

Quails with apples
SERVES 4

Bramleys are expensive at this time of year and instead I would use Discovery, the first of the new season's English apples.

4 quails
Salt and pepper
2 oz / 50 g butter

4 English apples, peeled and sliced
½ pint / 300 ml dry cider

Clean, wash and trim the quails, removing feet, head and neck. Salt and pepper inside. Heat half the butter in a shallow casserole or frying pan with a lid. Brown the quails all over and add half the cider, bring to the boil and simmer for 20–30 minutes, covered. When cooked, remove the quails from the sauce and keep them warm. Add the rest of the cider and reduce the sauce until fairly syrupy. Season to taste. In another shallow pan fry the slices of apple in the rest of the butter, and when tender divide among four heated plates. Serve the quails on top and surround with sauce.

Scalloped potatoes and green salad would round off the main course.

Caramel cream
SERVES 4

Vanilla pod
1 pint / 600 ml single cream
3 eggs

4 oz / 100 g sugar
2 tablespoons water

Bring the cream slowly to the boil with the vanilla pod. Meanwhile beat the eggs in a basin with 1 oz / 25 g sugar. Pour on the hot cream, whisking all the time. Remove the vanilla pod, wash and dry it for use again. In a small heavy saucepan melt the rest of the sugar in the water. When melted, raise the heat and allow to caramelise and go light brown. Then pour it into four individual ramekins or a soufflé dish, swirling the caramel round to cover the base and the sides of the ramekins. Strain the egg and cream mixture into the ramekins. Stand in a roasting tin containing a little water, and bake in a moderate oven for 25–30 minutes. You will know when it is ready by sticking a knife point into the centre of the cream – it will come out dry when cooked.

Allow to go cold, then refrigerate. To serve, unmould on to plates.

PARMA HAM WITH FRUIT
WILD DUCK WITH WILD RICE
CHINESE LEAVES
PLUMS BOURDALOUE

For those of us who love game but cannot afford grouse, September 1st is the day to look forward to – the opening of the duck season. Of course, no one would actually eat it there and then as it does need a good twenty-four hours to ripen off. In any case, you might not be lucky enough to bag any on the first day.

Château Gloria, Saint-Julien is one of our favourite clarets. We are enjoying the 1976 at the moment which should drink into the late 1980s. Younger vintages too will come into their own. Harvey's No. 1 Claret is a good alternative which we always find quite suitable when we cannot afford one more expensive.

Parma ham with fruit
SERVES 4

The success of this dish depends to a large extent on the fruit you use. It must be perfect – sweet and ripe and without blemish. I hope you can persuade your greengrocer to sell such a rarity. Melon or figs is the traditional accompaniment. I have often served it with papaya (paw paw) when I can find this at a reasonable price. However, one of the best fruits to go with the ham would be a perfect juicy pear, peeled and sliced, and chilled in the fridge.

8 oz / 225 g finely sliced Parma ham

Black pepper
Fruit

Arrange the ham on individual serving plates. Slice your chosen fruit and arrange decoratively around the ham. Grind fresh black pepper overall. Serve immediately.

Wild duck with wild rice
SERVES 4

These are small birds and to serve four people you will need two. With little meat on them, you may like to stretch the dish by stuffing them. Because the birds cook very quickly the stuffing should already be largely cooked.

Wild rice is a wonderful accompaniment to game. For me it has the same rare quality of having had to be hunted or sought for. In its natural state it grows as a tall, graceful grass in the lakes and wilderness of the northern central region of America and the adjoining areas of Canada. Traditionally it is harvested by the Indian nations. Because of its scarceness it is expensive, but 4 oz / 100 g is ample for four people as it swells to several times its dry volume. I generally prepare it in the same way as I do buttered rice, cooking it perhaps a little longer. It can be bought in Harrods, Selfridges, Fortnum and Mason and other good grocery shops. Relatives and friends in America send it from time to time, though it is expensive there too, and anybody visiting us from America is always instructed to slip a couple of half-pound packets into their suitcase.

2 wild duck	Seasoning
6–8 tablespoons cooked wild rice (or brown rice, if you cannot get wild rice)	Plenty of glossy watercress
	Quince or bramble jelly

Heat the oven to gas mark 6, 200°C / 400°F. Wipe the birds out and pull out any bits of feathers, or singe them off. Salt and pepper inside the cavity. Fill each one with the cooked rice and secure the cavity closed with a cocktail stick.

Place the birds on a rack in a roasting tin containing a few tablespoons of water. Any roasting juices will drop into the tin and together with the water will make a little light gravy. Put the tin in the oven and roast for 25–35 minutes depending on how well done you like your wild duck. We tend to like it quite rare and juicy. Remove the birds from the oven and allow to rest for a few minutes.

Carve the breasts and legs, a portion of each for each serving, and serve with watercress and a spoonful of quince or bramble jelly.

As to a vegetable, Chinese leaves are good at this time of year. Serve either as a salad, or shredded and stir-fried.

Victoria or Stanley plums are good in this dish.

Plums
Bourdaloue
SERVES 4–6

1½ lb / 700 g plums	*Almond Paste*
3–4 oz / 100–125 g almond paste	Makes 1 lb / 450 g
½ oz / 15 g butter	3½ oz / 100 g icing sugar
	3½ oz / 100 g castor sugar
	8 oz / 225 g ground almonds
	Lemon juice
	Beaten egg

Sift the icing sugar on to a pastry board. Add the castor sugar and ground almonds. Work in, with the fingers, sufficient lemon juice and beaten egg to make a stiff paste of a dough-like consistency.

Wash the plums. Make a long slit down one side and remove the stone. Mould a small piece of almond paste into the shape of the kernel and slip it into place in the plum. Stuff all the plums in this way.

Butter an ovenproof dish and put the plums in it in a single layer. Cover with foil and bake towards the bottom of a medium oven for 30 minutes. Alternatively, you can cook these, without butter, slowly on top of the stove in a non-stick frying pan.

They are rich, sticky and delicious to eat.

OXTAIL AND TOMATO SOUP
BAKED SEA BASS WITH LEEKS
LEMON AND BLACKBERRY SOUFFLÉ

A Gewürztraminer from Alsace, especially the 1976 vintage, would be fine throughout this meal.

Oxtail and
tomato soup
SERVES 4–6

1 lb / 450 g oxtail, cut into pieces	1 lb / 450 g ripe tomatoes
Seasoned flour	½ teaspoon dill seeds
2 onions	2 pints / 1 litre water
1 stick of celery	Seasoning

Shake the pieces of oxtail in a bag of seasoned flour. Seal them in a non-stick frying pan, then transfer them to a casserole. Peel and slice the onions. Trim and slice the celery. Cook the onions and celery until lightly browned. Roughly chop the tomatoes and add to the vegetables, with the dill seed. Bring to the boil and pour over the meat. Pour 1 pint / 500 ml water into the frying pan, bring to the boil and scrape off any bits. Add to the rest of the ingredients with the remaining water. Bring back to the boil. Cover and simmer, or put in a low oven, for 1½ hours.

When the meat is very tender and about to fall off the bone, remove the pieces of oxtail from the pot. When cool enough to handle, remove the meat from the bones and put to one side. Put the rest of the liquid, tomatoes etc. through a sieve, or put in the blender, process and then sieve, forcing through as much as possible. Put the sieved soup back in the pan, add some neatly trimmed pieces of oxtail. Season to taste and bring back to boiling point. Serve immediately.

If there is quite a bit of meat left, pound it up with an equal quantity of butter. Add salt and pepper to taste, and a little powdered mace or nutmeg, and use it as potted beef.

Baked sea bass
with leeks
SERVES 4

Ask your fishmonger to clean and scale the fish for you.

2½ lb / 1¼ kg sea bass   1 wineglass dry white wine
Seasoning   2 lb / 900 g leeks
2 oz / 50 g butter

Wash and dry the fish inside and out. Butter an oval, iron dish and place the fish in it. Season very lightly. Dot with a little more butter, pour on the wine and cover with foil or a butter paper. Bring to boiling point on top of the stove and then put in a hot oven for 15–20 minutes. Meanwhile trim and thoroughly wash the leeks. Slice them finely and then steam. When almost soft, melt the rest of the butter in a saucepan, stir in the leeks, and cook almost to a purée. Remove the fish from the oven and carefully lay it on an oval serving plate. Surround it with leek purée and serve separately the fishy cooking juices which you should reduce until syrupy.

Serve with a green salad.

1 oz / 25 g butter
1 oz / 25 g flour
½ pint / 300 ml milk
2 oz / 50 g castor sugar
2 lemons

3 whole eggs
1 egg white
4 dessertspoons blackberry
jam or purée

*Lemon and
blackberry
soufflé*
SERVES 4–5

Butter a 1½ pint / 850 ml soufflé dish. Melt the butter in a heavy pan, stir in the flour. When it is all absorbed pour in a little milk. Beat until smooth. Continue adding the milk, beating and returning to the boil. Boil gently for 5 minutes. Stir in the sugar and the grated zest of two lemons. Cut one of the lemons in half and squeeze the juice into the white sauce. Mix thoroughly. Remove from heat and cool slightly.

Separate the eggs and beat the yolks, one at a time, into the lemon mixture. Whisk the egg whites until soft and fold these into the mixture. Pour into the prepared soufflé dish and bake in the oven at gas mark 4, 180°C / 350°F, for 25 minutes.

To serve, heat the jam or purée. Break open the top of the soufflé which will be lightly browned and well risen, and pour the hot sauce into the middle.

TAGLIOLINI, QUAIL EGGS & MUSHROOMS
PORK WITH LEMON & WATERCRESS SAUCE
SALAD
MUSCAT GRAPE TART

A red Rioja, preferably a *riserva* with a few years' bottle age – the older the better, says Tom, thinking of our 1955 Viña Pomal which has long since disappeared from wine lists and shelves. We are still guarding one bottle.

This is a very effective and pleasing dinner party dish; the eggs sit in a 'nest' of fresh pasta and are accompanied by a small amount of rich sauce. If quail eggs are not available you could use other good things – queen scallops, prawns, mussels, sweetbreads, tiny fresh vegetables – and adjust the sauce accordingly. You wouldn't use a meat stock if you were preparing shellfish, and would use vegetable stock if you were preparing the dish for vegetarians. If you cannot get wild

*Tagliolini,
quail eggs &
mushrooms*
SERVES 4

mushrooms use instead the same quantity of button or cup mushrooms. See p. 25 for homemade pasta.

½ lb / 225 g fresh, homemade
   or packet tagliolini
4 oz / 125 g fresh wild
   mushrooms
½ oz / 15 g dried wild
   mushrooms
1 dozen quail eggs

1 oz / 25 g butter
1 shallot or small onion, finely
   chopped
¼ pint / 150 ml good stock
¼ pint / 150 ml double cream
Seasoning to taste

Put the dried mushrooms to soak in water for at least 30 minutes and preferably 2 hours before you need them.

Prepare the quail eggs by putting them in a pan of cold water, bring to the boil, remove from the heat and leave standing for half a minute. Run cold water into the pan for a moment to cool the eggs enough for you to shell them, which you should do immediately, placing them then in warm water to keep warm until ready to serve. It is important to have the eggs soft-boiled, but difficult to get them just right. Make the sauce by softening the onion or shallot in the butter, add both lots of mushrooms and cook briefly. Add the stock and reduce by half. Add the cream, reduce further for a couple of minutes. Season to taste and keep warm.

Cook the pasta according to the directions. Drain. Arrange into nests on individual serving plates, with three quail eggs in each, surround with a little sauce and a few pieces of mushroom.

Pork with lemon & watercress sauce
SERVES 4

You will probably have served little or no pork during the summer, so now is the time to start enjoying it again. More often than not, it is served with fruit – apple sauce or prunes – but I like also to serve it with a sharper sauce, particularly since the rest of the meal is quite rich.

1¼ lb / 550 g fillet of pork, also
   known as tenderloin
1 lemon
½–1 teaspoon crushed
   coriander, cumin or
   cardamom seeds
½ pint / 300 ml veal or chicken
   stock

Bunch of watercress (leaves
   only, save the stalks for
   soup)
Tablespoon of *fromage frais* or
   thick yoghurt

Cut the fillet into slices about 1 in / 25 mm thick and flatten slightly. Grate zest from half the lemon and squeeze the juice from the same half over the pork. Add the spices. Leave to marinate for an hour or two. You can, at this point if you wish, add a little crushed garlic.

Heat a non-stick frying pan. Dry the *noisettes* and place in a single layer in the heated pan. As soon as the first side is sealed and lightly brown, turn over and seal the other side, maintaining a high heat. This part of the operation takes less than a minute a side. When browned on the second side, lower the heat as far as possible. Add the juice of the other half lemon, reserving the grated zest, and half the stock. Simmer gently, uncovered, until tender – about 25 minutes. Remove the meat and keep it warm while you finish the sauce. Add the rest of the stock, reduce slightly and season to taste. Finely chop the watercress leaves and stir into the sauce. Cook for a minute or less, lower the heat, stir in the *fromage frais*, *quark* or thick yoghurt and heat through but don't let it bubble as it might well separate. Serve the *noisettes* on top of the sauce.

To accompany the pork I would return to tradition and serve some boiled potatoes.

Muscat grape tart
SERVES 4–6

Muscat grapes from Italy are now imported almost right through to Christmas. Choose those that are most golden, even those with occasional brown flecks on the skin, for the most pronounced muscat scent and flavour. Unfortunately, I see many greengrocers advertising as *muscat* grapes that are not muscat at all. If you are brave, ask if you can taste one. The muscat flavour is unmistakable.

This is rather a fiddly dish to prepare since you should peel the grapes and remove the pips, but worth it for a special occasion. The pastry base can be made well in advance.

I recently came across a pastry recipe which breaks all the rules and which I now use for most of my soft fruit tarts. It was told to me by Sheila Clark, a gifted, inventive cook who lives in Kent. I first tasted it smothered with whipped cream and local raspberries.

Pastry
5 oz / 150 g butter
2½ oz / 75 g sugar, or less, to taste
About 8 oz / 225 g plain flour

Melt the butter gently in a heavy saucepan. Add the sugar and let it melt and amalgamate but not cook. Remove from the heat. Then, in the pan, begin to work in the flour. The mixture will eventually become a stiff dough. Press it with your fingers or the back of a wooden spoon into a buttered baking dish, tin or ring on a base. Prick all over and bake for 12–15 minutes at gas mark 6, 200°C / 400°F moving it to a lower shelf if it shows signs of burning.

Peel and deseed and chill ¾ lb / 350 g muscat grapes. As they are so large it won't seem quite such a tiresome chore; after all, you peel small tomatoes.

When the base is cool and you are almost ready to serve the tart, spread on it a layer of very cold whipped cream or thick yoghurt or soft white cheese (*fromage blanc*) and cover with the grapes. Slice and serve, accompanied by a glass of chilled muscat wine or, for the purists, a Barsac of a not too grand year or address.

TORTELLINI DI ZUCCA
GRATIN OF FISH FLORENTINE
SALAD
CHEESE
MELON

We tasted *tortellini di zucca* (little pasta parcels stuffed with pumpkin) for the first time in Mantova and for the rest of our stay in the Emilia Romagna region ate it sometimes twice a day looking for the best version. As so often happens, the first dish was the best. It was one of the many regional specialities we enjoyed at Il Cigno in Mantova, a restaurant highly acclaimed in *I Ristorante di Veronelli*, the best guide to Italian restaurants. It took some time to work out what went into the pasta besides pumpkin, but I think I now have a version as close to the original as possible.

An Italian white wine would be right here, I think. If you can find it, a Prosecco, a dry sparkling wine from the Valdobbiadene or Conegliano in the Veneto would be nice. Otherwise, I might choose a Soave.

A good-sized chunk of fresh pumpkin weighing about 1¼ lb / 600 g will cook down to about 4 oz / 125 g of firm packed pumpkin. Or you can buy it tinned. *Mostarda* is an Italian speciality from Cremona which can be bought in well-stocked Italian grocers' or delicatessens. It is preserved fruit in a clear, mustardy syrup which is often served with the *bollito misto*, mixed boiled meats. As a substitute I have used thick apricot jam mixed with mustard, in equal quantities. It occurs to me that mango chutney might be an appropriate alternative.

Tortellini di zucca
SERVES 4
AS A STARTER,
2 AS A
MAIN COURSE

For the pasta
5 oz / 150 g plain flour
2 oz / 50 g fine semolina
2 size-3 eggs

For the filling
4 oz / 125 g pumpkin purée
1 oz / 25 g freshly grated Parmesan
1 oz / 25 g ground almonds
1 tablespoon finely chopped *mostarda*
Freshly ground nutmeg, to taste.

Mix the pasta ingredients in a food processor, or by hand in a bowl or on a marble work surface. Roll out thin sheets of dough.

Mix together the ingredients for the filling. Place spoonfuls of filling at regular intervals on one sheet of dough. Run a damp pastry brush along the spaces, cover with another sheet of dough, pressing down around the filling. Stamp out circles with a pastry cutter or special pasta cutter. Allow the pasta to dry on a board covered with a teatowel. Turn once during drying time. Drop into a large pan of boiling salted water and boil rapidly for 4 minutes. Drain.

This is a time-consuming dish to prepare but worth the effort. And it can be prepared well in advance. I have even let it dry overnight and served it for lunch the next day. No rich sauces are served with *tortellini di zucca*, simply melted butter in which you have heated a sprig of rosemary or sage, and a final scattering of fresh nutmeg. The dish should have quite a pronounced nutmeg flavour.

One of my favourite autumn and winter dishes is a raw fish salad. I use whatever fish is fresh in the market that day, lightly marinated in vodka and onions for an hour or so before serving. (See p. 53.) I would be reluctant to ask even the best-disposed fishmonger for 3 oz

Gratin of fish florentine
SERVES 4 AS A
MAIN COURSE,
6 AS A STARTER

of this and 3 oz of that so I usually buy a cutlet of salmon, a sole fillet, ½ lb monkfish etc. This leaves me with quite a lot of fish. I marinate it all, and use it in a baked dish the next day which is delicious and tastes nothing like you imagine leftovers to taste. Because I use such fine quality fish in the salad, this *gratin* becomes rather a grand dish in its own right.

6 oz / 175 g sole fillet	1 lb / 450 g freshly steamed
Piece of salmon	spinach
A monkfish tail	½ pint / 300 ml light white
Some pieces of scallop and	sauce
their roe	2 oz / 50 g grated cheese,
1 oz / 25 g butter	Gruyère for preference

Butter an ovenproof dish. Cover the base with spinach. Cut the fish into similar sized pieces, perhaps wrapping a strip of sole around a piece of scallop coral to prevent it from overcooking. Dry the fish very thoroughly and place it in a single layer on top of the spinach. Add any marinade including the thinly sliced onions to the white sauce and then stir in the grated cheese. Pour the sauce over the fish and bake in a hot oven gas mark 6, 200°C / 400°F, for 8–10 minutes.

Follow this with a crisp salad, then a little cheese, and nothing more than fresh, chilled fruit. At this time of year you will still find good honeydew melons about.

FISH SOUP
CHICKEN BREASTS WITH PRESERVED FRUIT
JULIENNE OF LEEKS
YOGHURT AND HONEY WITH ALMONDS

If your fishmonger is generous with his fish pieces you will find this a relatively inexpensive meal. But if you can only get heads and bones, then you will need to buy some fish as well. Although quantities are given for four, this is an easy meal to do for larger numbers. A big pot of soup is just as simple to make as a small one, and it takes no longer to cook six or eight chicken breasts than it does four. It does require, of course, more preparation time.

A young Muscadet-Sur-Lie is the classic wine to serve with a fish soup and is widely available at reasonable prices. Château de la Casse-michère is one we have particularly enjoyed. Why not drink it with the chicken as well?

Fish soup
SERVES 4–6

Tell your fishmonger that you want bones and pieces for soup and he will give you the right things – i.e. no mackerel or herring or other oily fish. Salmon heads are excellent but there is usually a charge for these. Monkfish bones are good, as are plaice, sole and turbot.

You may be able to trim quite a lot off the pieces but if not, buy a mixture of fish, depending on how much you want to spend, from coley, pollock and whiting, up to salmon, turbot and sole. A few prawns, mussels or scallops add extra flavour.

2–3 lb / 1–1½ kg fish bones and
   pieces
1 carrot
1 onion
1 celery stalk
1 lb / 450 g fish, off the bone
2 tablespoons olive oil
2 sliced onions

2 crushed garlic cloves
1 medium-sized fennel bulb
Pinch of saffron or turmeric
½ lb / 225 g fresh tomatoes,
   peeled and deseeded or small
   tin of tomatoes
Seasoning to taste

Make up a stock using the fish bones, chopped carrot, celery and onion and 4 pints / 2¼ l of water. Simmer for an hour, strain. In a large heavy pot heat the oil and cook the onion and garlic without letting them burn. Slice or chop the fennel, setting aside any feathery tops for garnish, and add to the onion and garlic. Cook the fennel for five minutes then add the tomatoes, crushing with a wooden spoon as you add them to the pan. Cook the vegetables until almost soft and then add the stock. Allow to reduce a little. Take two tablespoons of the broth and place it in a teacup with the saffron. Let it steep for a few minutes then return it all to the pan. If you are using turmeric, blend it into a little stock in a teacup and add it to the broth.

Cut the fish into bite-sized pieces and add to the broth shortly before you are ready to serve. Small pieces of fish will take no more than a few seconds to cook, and will go on cooking in the hot soup once you've turned off the heat.

Serve very hot, in heated soup bowls. Fish soup is traditionally served in the south of France (and almost everywhere else now) with *croûtons*, grated cheese (which should be a good Gruyère) and a garlicky, peppery *rouille* which you can make by adding cayenne pepper, paprika and a spot of tomato purée to a very garlicky mayonnaise.

This is a very filling soup and can quite happily be served as a main course followed by salad, cheese and fruit. A less filling version served in smaller quantities is made by adding only 8 oz / 225 g white fish and putting the whole lot through the blender, producing a smooth amber-coloured soup. Don't forget to garnish with fennel.

Chicken breasts with preserved fruit
SERVES 4

4 chicken breasts
4 tablespoons brown
  breadcrumbs
1 oz / 25 g butter
Crushed garlic – to taste
Salt and pepper

2 tablespoons *mostarda*, finely
  chopped (see p. 25)
4 circles of greaseproof paper,
  each large enough to take
  one chicken breast

Cook the chicken breasts quickly in a non-stick frying pan. Cool quickly and split lengthwise, but not all the way through. Stuff this cavity with the breadcrumbs, butter, garlic, seasoning and fruit all combined together. Secure the two flaps together with half a toothpick. Lightly oil or butter the greaseproof paper. Lay a chicken breast on one half, fold the other half over so that the edges meet. Fold over the edges tightly, twisting them as you work all round the half circle. This will ensure an airtight seal. Place the parcels on a baking tray and bake in the middle of a pre-heated oven gas mark 4, 180°C / 350°F, for 30–35 minutes.

Serve each person with a parcel on their dinner plate, which they unwrap themselves, together with a *julienne* of leeks. You prepare these by washing the leeks carefully and cutting them into shreds, then lightly steaming them. A spoonful of bramble or quince jelly would look pretty on the plate as well as enhancing the flavour of the dish.

Small baked potatoes could be served if you remember to put them in the oven well before the chicken.

Fresh fruit and cheese is all you will need at the end of this substantial meal – or greek yoghurt with almonds and clear honey spooned over it.

ARTICHOKES VINAIGRETTE
VEGETABLE CRUMBLE
WALNUT SALAD
MARRON SOUFFLÉ

As a non-vegetarian, I find cooking for vegetarians can be quite daunting. Even more daunting though, for a non-vegetarian, is to presume to write about a vegetarian meal. On the one occasion in the past when I did so, I received one letter complaining about my use of cream and another complaining that I had used too many vegetables and that it was a fallacy to assume that vegetarians ate a lot of vegetables. Since we eat plenty of vegetables in our everyday meals I am not too worried about continuing to serve them when we entertain friends who are vegetarians. What is important, I think, is to get a balance in the methods of cooking used. I wouldn't want to serve a *gougère* followed by a quiche followed by a soufflé or a mousse as was suggested to me by one correspondent. Such a meal would give little variety, either to the cook or to the diner. The meal I give here then is not intended as a blue-print for a vegetarian life-style, but simply the sort of meal I would cook if vegetarians were coming to dinner. And indeed the sort of meal I often cook for the two of us alone.

Artichokes change the flavour of wine. But with the main course how about a nice Beaujolais – a Moulin-à-Vent or a Chiroubles? Look for 1976 or 1978 which are going to last a while. The older the better for Moulin-à-Vent. On the other hand, this is the time of year when 'le Beaujolais Nouveau est arrivé'.

These are best served when cool, not just out of the refrigerator. Remove the outside leaves, particularly if they are bruised, but I see little reason to snip off the points of the leaves. But it does make sense to leave some of the stalk on (if it is young and tender), peeling off the outside fibrous part and rubbing the inner stalk with lemon juice. This is as tasty and tender as the artichoke heart.

Artichokes vinaigrette

Plunge the artichokes into boiling water and cook until done. The time will depend upon size and age – anything from 20–50 minutes.

Serve with your favourite vinaigrette. I have a rather unorthodox one which is particularly good with vegetables but can also be used on a fairly robust salad. Large quantities can be made in a blender or food processor, smaller quantities shaken in a jar.

6 parts good olive oil
1 part white wine vinegar, flavoured wine vinegar, rice vinegar or lemon juice
A splash or two of some or all of the following:

French mustard
Angostura bitters
Soy sauce
Worcester sauce
Tomato ketchup
Salt, pepper

To which add, if you wish, crushed garlic, crushed walnuts or pinenuts, freshly chopped fresh herbs.

Vegetable crumble
SERVES 4–5

This is basically a *ratatouille* with a crumble topping. By now the courgettes are rather large and past their best, so they are just as well combined with other ingredients – aubergines, tomatoes, peppers etc. of which there are plenty available.

Ratatouille
1 lb / 450 g aubergines
1 lb / 450 g courgettes
1 large green pepper
1 onion
1 lb / 450 g tomatoes
Garlic – to taste
Seasoning
Olive oil

Crumble
6 oz / 150 g plain flour
3 oz / 75 g butter or margarine
1 oz / 25 g freshly grated Parmesan
1 tablespoon finely chopped fresh herbs or 1 teaspoon finely ground dried herbs

Cut the aubergine into chunks. Sprinkle with salt and let it disgorge for an hour to get rid of any bitter taste. I have found with very young small aubergines that this process is unnecessary. Rinse and dry well. Meanwhile slice the courgettes into ½ in / 1 cm pieces. Slice the green pepper and the onion. Skin, deseed and roughly chop the tomatoes. Crush the garlic with a little salt.

Heat the olive oil in a casserole, about three tablespoons to begin with, though you may need to add more later. Stir in all the vegetables, on a fairly high heat, until well-coated with oil. Add the garlic and a pinch of pepper. Remember that the aubergine will have absorbed some salt and that you crushed the garlic with salt, so you should not require any more salt in this dish.

Cook gently in their own juices, either in the oven or on top of the stove, until all the vegetables are tender, but not breaking up into a purée. Transfer the ratatouille to an ovenproof dish that will also look well on the table.

To make the crumble, rub the fat into the flour with the tips of the fingers until it resembles breadcrumbs or, even better, make it in the food processor. Mix in the fresh herbs. Spoon the crumble over the ratatouille and press down lightly. Sprinkle the Parmesan over the top and bake for about 15 minutes at gas mark 6, 200°C/400°F.

Accompany it with a plain green salad to which you have added a few walnuts and dressed simply with walnut oil and lemon juice.

For this dish, buying a tin of chestnut purée from the Ardèche, now sold in many delicatessens, is much, much easier than peeling, cooking and pounding fresh chestnuts which I find a tiresome and painful chore, resulting in burnt fingers and bad tempers.

Marron soufflé
SERVES 4

6 oz/175 g unsweetened
   chestnut purée
2 tablespoons of honey
A drop or two of vanilla

2 egg yolks
4 egg whites
4 dessertspoons whipped
   cream

Butter four small ramekins and set in a roasting tin containing ½ in/1 cm water. Mix the purée with the honey, vanilla and egg yolks very thoroughly. Whisk the egg whites to firm peaks and fold into the chestnut mixture. Fill the ramekins to within ¼ in/5 mm of the top, place in a pre-heated oven gas mark 4, 180°C/350°F, and bake for 15–20 minutes. Serve immediately. Crack open the top of each soufflé and spoon the whipped cream into it.

MARINATED CARROTS
FISH CHOWDER
GREEN SALAD
SPICED BLACKBERRY CRUMBLE

This is a tasty, inexpensive meal, with plenty of colour and contrast. I would serve a good, dry French cider with this meal. You might prefer English cider – equally good as long as it is dry.

Marinated carrots
SERVES 4–6

1 lb / 450 g firm carrots
4 tablespoons olive oil
1 tablespoon lemon juice, wine vinegar or fruit vinegar
1 teaspoon chopped fresh herbs

3 crushed cloves garlic
Salt
Pepper
2 mild sweet onions

Peel or scrape the carrots and slice them very thinly. Drop into boiling water or put in a steamer basket and cook for 1–2 minutes.

Mix the oil, vinegar, herbs, garlic and seasoning. Peel and thinly slice the onions. Drain the carrots and toss them while still hot in the dressing. Arrange the onion slices on individual plates and spoon the carrots on top. Serve while still warm, or when cold.

Fish chowder
SERVES 4

¼ lb / 100 g smoked streaky bacon
4 medium onions
4 potatoes
1 pint / 600 ml fish stock
2 tablespoons finely chopped parsley

1 lb / 450 g white fish fillets – cod, plaice, and monkfish are all suitable
4 oz / 120 g unsweetened, natural yoghurt

Cut the bacon into strips and render it in a heavy casserole. Peel and slice the onions and potatoes and add to the bacon. Cook, without letting them brown, for 10 minutes or so until the vegetables are softening. Add the fish stock and simmer for 10 minutes. Cut the fish into fairly large chunks and add to the stock, with the parsley. Simmer for no more than 5 minutes. Mix a little of the liquid with the yoghurt to form a thin cream and pour this back into the pot, without letting it boil any more. Serve very hot with crusty bread and follow with a crisp green salad.

Spiced blackberry crumble
SERVES 4–6

1½ lb / 700 g ripe blackberries
5 oz / 125 g plain flour
3 oz / 75 g butter

2 oz / 50 g castor sugar
1 teaspoon ground cinnamon and nutmeg, mixed

Wash and drain the blackberries. Pour into a buttered pie plate. Rub the flour and butter together until crumb-like. (This is most easily done in a food processor.) Fold in the sugar and spices. Sprinkle the blackberries with a tablespoon of water. Spoon the crumble topping over the blackberries to cover them and press it down lightly. Bake in the oven at gas mark 6, 200°C/400°F, for 20 minutes.

BLINIS
VEAL SKOBLIANKA
SALAD
FIG SORBET

Blinis are a traditional Russian dish – small pancakes made with a yeast batter to be served with melted butter and sour cream and topped with caviar. We first came across them at Dominique, a Franco-Russian restaurant full of tsarist atmosphere in Montparnasse. Although the food is not what it once was, in my view it is still fun to go there late at night for a supper of *zakouskis* (*hors d'oeuvres*), *blinis* (without the caviar) and a small carafe of the purest, most delicious vodka set in a bucket of ice, and to pretend you are surrounded by spies and *agents provocateurs*.

Dominique serves a veal dish which I like very much, called *skoblianka* and similar to the French *blanquette de veau*. Their *shashliks* are very impressive, swords speared full of meat chunks brought flaming into the dining room, so perhaps not for the domestic scene. To finish we are usually offered Russian cheesecake or a *tarte maison* which is a little heavy after such a meal, so I would serve a sorbet instead, with fresh figs if I could get them.

If this is to be a special dinner, why not serve a Condrieu, the white Rhône wine made in small quantities (though not as small as Château-Grillet) from the Viognier grape. Choose as young a vintage as possible, provided it is a good one, and from a good grower such as Guigal.

The traditional Russian recipe calls for buckwheat, but I have often used self-raising flour, or a mixture of this and wholemeal.

Blinis
SERVES 4–6

½ pint/300 ml milk and water mixed	4 oz/125 g flour
1 level teaspoon dried yeast	1 egg
	Pinch salt

Accompaniments: Melted butter, sour cream, lemon quarters
Topping: Some or all of the following: smoked salmon pieces, smoked fish pâté, smoked cod's roe, salmon roe, lumpfish roe, red and black, and, of course, caviar if you wish

Heat the liquid to blood heat. Pour a quarter of it into a cup and sprinkle the yeast on top. Let it work for 10 minutes or so, then beat it into the rest of the ingredients. Allow to prove for 30–40 minutes, making sure that the container is large enough as the yeast will make the batter 'grow'.

Heat a non-stick frying pan. A large one will make about four blinis at a time. A soupspoon of batter makes just the right size. Spoon the batter into the pan. It will be quite thick and will not spread much. Cook until the surface dries and bubbles. Turn over and cook the other side for a minute. Remove to a plate standing on a pan of hot water. Continue until all the batter is used up.

Ideally you should pass the pancakes to your guests as soon as they are cooked. They then help themselves to melted butter, sour cream and the topping of their choice. Iced vodka really is the perfect drink with this, served in glasses which have spent some time in the freezer. Only the best vodka will do, Polish or Russian, Swedish or Finnish.

Veal skoblianka
SERVES 4–6

If you can, buy your veal in a whole piece. It is much easier to trim a large piece than a lot of small chunks.

1½ lbs / 700 g lean pie veal	¼ pint / 150 ml stock
1 oz / 25 g butter	1 tablespoon cream
7 small onions	1 egg
4 cloves	Parsley
1 lemon	

Trim the veal and cut it into chunks. In a casserole melt the butter and seal the meat without letting it brown. Peel the onions and stick the cloves into one of them. Gently fry the onions. Grate the zest from the lemon and add this to the meat, together with the lemon juice and stock. Cover and simmer very gently until tender. About 50 minutes should be enough. When done, strain the juices into a small saucepan and boil to reduce. Season to taste. Beat the egg and cream. Add a little hot meat sauce and return the whole to the rest of the sauce, taking care not to let it boil which will curdle it, but still keeping it hot. Arrange the veal on a serving dish and pour the sauce over it. Garnish with parsley and serve with rice.

1 lb / 450 g fresh figs or soaked dried figs
1 pint / 600 ml freshly made jasmin or green tea

2 tablespoons honey
Seeds of 3 cardamom pods

Fig sorbet
SERVES 4–6

Poach the figs in the tea, honey and cardamom until soft. Cool, then make into a purée, sieving if necessary, chill and freeze. Stir from time to time, unless using a *sorbetière* or ice cream maker.

GARLIC SOUP
CASSEROLE OF HARE
AUBERGINE CREAM
NUT PIE

There is a painting by Velázquez in the National Gallery of Scotland showing a woman concentrating on the preparation of food in a dark kitchen, watched, if I remember correctly, by a young boy. I like to think that she is preparing *sopa de ajo*, also called Castilian soup.

This is easy to make. Cheap, nourishing and delicious. The most important thing about the preparation is that your soup bowls must be ovenproof, as the soup is baked and served almost too hot to eat.

If you have a reliable wine merchant or other source of wine, ask him to recommend a red burgundy. I would serve the Wine Society's red burgundy, full-bodied, smooth and easy to drink. The Hungarian Tokay, still very good value in the half-litre bottles, goes particularly well with nut pie. Buy the sweetest – 5 puttonyos – if you can get it.

4 teaspoons good olive oil
1½ pints / 900 ml light stock
4–8 cloves of garlic, crushed
4 eggs
3 or 4 thickish slices of day-old, white bread

2 oz / 50 g smoked bacon, cured or smoked ham, chopped or shredded – optional

Garlic soup
SERVES 4

Put a teaspoon of olive oil in each bowl and place in a hot oven for 5 minutes. Heat the stock to boiling point. Lightly fry the ham or bacon if you are using it. Remove the soup bowls from the oven. Carefully crack an egg into each bowl, pour on the hot stock, add the crushed garlic, ham and the bread broken into ½ in / 1 cm chunks. Return the bowls to the oven for another 2–3 minutes. Longer will not be necessary because the egg begins to set as soon as it meets the heat of the soup bowl, and the hot stock sets it some more. Serve while still bubbling hot, setting the bowls on serving plates.

This soup, as made in Castile, is more often than not simply a mixture of olive oil and water, in which case you need to increase the proportion of oil. I prefer it less oily and have suggested stock.

Casserole of hare
SERVES 4

Hare is at its best in October and this is a good way of using up joints after you've roasted the saddle at another meal. It is a dish that should be cooked slowly and so is suitable for use with the automatic oven; delicious to come home to in the evening, all ready to dish up.

Fore and hind legs of a good-sized hare

For the marinade	*For cooking*
1 sliced onion	1 tablespoon
1 carrot, chopped	*eau-de-vie-de-poire*
1 stick of celery, chopped	1 onion
2 crushed cloves of garlic	2 sticks of celery
6 crushed juniper berries	1 tablespoon olive oil or butter
1 teaspoon of whole allspice	1 oz / 25 g seasoned flour
¼ pint / 150 ml red wine	4 dried pears
or wine glass of port	¼ pint / 150 ml hare stock
or ¼ pint / 150 ml apple or	Parsley
orange juice	
1 tablespoon olive oil	
1 sprig of rosemary	
Zest of half a lemon	

Wash and wipe dry the pieces of hare. Place in a bowl. Heat all the marinade ingredients to boiling point. Cool to blood heat and pour over the hare. Leave to marinate overnight.

Next day dry the hare. Strain and reserve the marinade. Slice the onion and celery and fry to light brown in the olive oil or butter in a heavy casserole. Put the seasoned flour in a paper bag and shake the pieces of meat, one at a time, to coat them with flour. Shake off any surplus flour and cook so that each piece is lightly browned all over. Pour in the strained marinade, add the pieces of dried pear and the stock. Cover and cook in a low oven gas mark 3, 170°C/325°F, for 2½–3 hours. When tender, place the pieces of hare and pear on a serving dish. Reduce the sauce vigorously, add the *eau-de-vie* and pour over the meat. Garnish with parsley and serve with baked onions and aubergine cream.

You can, of course, use fresh pears but if you do, you should add them for the last 20–30 minutes of cooking time. They would otherwise disintegrate.

Aubergine cream

SERVES 4–6
OR MORE AS A
COLD STARTER
OR DIP

1 lb/450 g aubergine
Salt
Tablespoon olive oil

4 oz/125 g thick yoghurt – greek if you can get it

Slice the aubergine and sprinkle with salt. Let stand for 30 minutes, then rinse and dry. Oil an ovenproof dish and put a layer of aubergine on the bottom. Cover with a few spoonfuls of yoghurt. Add another layer of aubergines and finish with yoghurt. Cover with foil and bake in a low oven for 1½ hours by which time it will be almost a purée. Sprinkle with parsley.

Nut pie

SERVES 6–8

This is based on an old pecan pie recipe which I came across in the *Williamsburg Art of Cookery*, a collection of recipes taken or adapted from the first American cookery book, printed in Williamsburg in 1742. Because I have increased the quantity of nuts used, I have been able to cut down on the sugar and syrup.

Together with wild rice, pecans are occasionally brought for us by visitors from America. Otherwise you can use fresh filberts, almonds or walnuts. In October the first of the wet walnuts are available. They can sometimes be bitter, so work well in this very sweet pie.

8 oz/225 g short pastry
3 eggs
2 oz/50 g soft brown sugar
4 oz/100 g melted butter

4 oz/100 g corn syrup or Golden Syrup
Juice and zest of a lemon
10 oz/275 g shelled nuts

Roll out the pastry and line a tart tin or china baking dish. Bake blind in a hottish oven for 10 minutes. Remove and allow to cool. Beat the eggs with sugar, butter and syrup. When thoroughly mixed, beat in the lemon juice and grated zest. Put most of the nuts in the pie crust, saving about 2 oz / 50 g. Pour the filling on top and bake in the oven at gas mark 3–4, 175°C / 350°F, for 45 minutes. Ten minutes before the end, or before the filling is quite set, arrange the rest of the nuts on top of the pie, and continue baking.

TERRINE OF SWEETBREADS
CASSEROLE OF PIGEONS WITH WALNUTS
PURÉE OF CELERIAC AND POTATOES
ORANGE AND ALMOND PUDDING

This is a fairly elaborate meal, one which I would contemplate only if I had plenty of preparation time.

It is the sort of meal at which I would serve our 1966 Château Lynch-Moussas. Alternatives would be *petits châteaux* from the Graves or Pomerol of some of the more recent good vintages which are drinking now, such as 1979.

Terrine of
sweetbreads
SERVES 8

1 lb / 450 g calves' sweetbreads
6 oz / 175 g lean veal
6 oz / 175 g chicken breasts
2 egg whites
2 tablespoons *crème fraîche* or
   double cream

Salt, pepper, nutmeg
2 tablespoons finely chopped
   coriander

Soak the sweetbreads in a bowl of water to which you have added ½ teaspoonful of salt for at least half an hour. Change the water once or twice. Place the sweetbreads in a pan of cold water. Bring slowly to the boil and simmer for two to three minutes. Drain. Rinse in cold water and press the sweetbreads between two plates, weighting the top plate. When cold and pressed, remove any loose bits of fat, gristle and membrane. Set aside in a cool place.

Put the veal and chicken through a mincer or food processor twice and then through a sieve, moistening occasionally with egg white.

This is a laborious job and the best implements are a flat sieve (*tamis*) and a scraper. Once you have a soft mass of meat, mix in the rest of the egg white, the *crème fraîche*, salt, pepper and nutmeg to taste. The coriander is as much for decoration as for taste, so you can either mix it in with the veal and chicken *farce* or roll the pieces of sweetbread in it, which will give a pretty green outline in each slice.

To assemble, cut the sweetbreads into two or three long strips. Oil a 1 lb / 450 g loaf tin, line with greaseproof or wet it. Spread a layer of *farce* in the bottom and along the sides of the loaf tin. Place the strips of sweetbreads along the length; fill the spaces between with the *farce* and cover with the rest of the veal and chicken *farce*. Tap the loaf tin firmly on the edge of your work surface to settle the mixture and make sure there are no air pockets. Cover with foil and bake in a pre-heated oven gas mark 4, 180°C / 350°F, for about 40 minutes. Remove, allow to cool, and unmould on to a carving board. Serve warm or cold, sliced, with your favourite sauce and a leaf or two of salad.

The sauce you serve with this should be assertive in colour but not taste which would overpower the delicate flavour of the terrine. Mild red peppers, charred, skinned, lightly boiled and then puréed make a perfect sauce. Prepare this just before serving as it has a tendency to separate.

Casserole of pigeons with walnuts
SERVES 4

4 wood pigeons
1 pint / 600 ml of water
1 carrot
1 onion
1 celery stick
Bunch of parsley
3 shallots
3 cloves of garlic
½ bottle of red Bordeaux
2 oz / 50 g butter
½ lb / 225 g mushrooms (cèpes, button mushrooms, chanterelles, morilles or field mushrooms as available)
¼ lb / 125 g walnut halves shelled (wet walnuts if available)
Salt
Pepper

Stock
In one pint / 600 ml of water simmer for 45 minutes chopped onion, carrot, celery and parsley with the pigeon carcasses. Strain. At the same time, reduce the wine by half.

Casserole

Roast the pigeon breasts and legs in a very hot oven for 10 minutes. Lightly fry the chopped shallots and garlic in 1 oz / 25 g of butter in a heavy enamel or iron casserole. Add the pigeons, stock and wine, and cook in a medium oven for 25 minutes. Fifteen minutes before the end of cooking time add the mushrooms, which will have first been quickly browned in the rest of the butter, and the shelled walnuts. Check sauce for flavour. You may wish to drain it into another saucepan and reduce it if it is still a little thin. Only season right at the end of the cooking process. Serve on individual hot plates, with a spoonful or two of celeriac purée. Chopped parsley can be used as garnish to relieve the rich, dark appearance of the dish.

A crisp salad of Florentine fennel dressed in nothing more than a little olive oil, a squeeze of lemon juice and plenty of freshly ground black pepper will add just the right amount of contrasting texture.

A purée of celeriac and potatoes
SERVES 4–6

1 lb / 450 g old potatoes
1 medium-sized celeriac root
2 large heads of garlic
1 oz / 25 g butter
2 tablespoons single cream
Salt
Pepper

Peel the potatoes, celeriac and garlic. Cut the first two into chunks. Bring all to the boil in lightly salted water and simmer until soft. Drain and mash with butter and cream. Serve with the pigeons.

Orange and almond pudding
SERVES 4–5

The amaretto is optional but adding this almond liqueur makes the pudding particularly delicious.

4 oz / 100 g castor sugar
1 oz / 25 g sifted flour
3 oz / 75 g ground almonds
4 oz / 100 g butter
4 egg yolks, well beaten
Grated rind of one orange
Juice of one orange mixed
  with 2 tablespoons amaretto
A few flaked almonds

Beat all the ingredients together. Pour into a buttered charlotte or soufflé mould. Sprinkle on the almonds and bake in a medium hot oven for 30–40 minutes, depending on the depth of your baking dish.

This is also very good baked in an uncooked pastry shell.

BREAD

It is a common enough experience to realise, as adults, that when we were children we often knew what day of the week it was simply from the smells wafting through the house. My childhood was no exception. Friday is the day I remember best. Baking day. Apart from making wonderful light pastry tarts, rich fruit cakes, feathery sponges, my mother would bake (and still bakes) the bread to last until the next Friday. This would be two large tin loaves, and the one I liked best, the one we always ate first, a plait, curved, floury and golden. Only in retrospect do I appreciate it fully, of course. My brother and I took this wonderful food for granted. Sometimes the homemade bread would be finished before next baking day so one of us would be sent down to the village shop for a large white loaf. I loved it! My mother didn't. Shop bread was definitely second-best. Once, I remember, I nibbled the bread all the way home, and had eaten away all the crisp edges and corners. I suppose my brother used to go after that.

Bread can be a very nostalgic food, evoking precise memories of times and places. Though a cliché, it is one of the things I remember about my first visit to Paris, my first meals in cheap left bank bistros as a student. And when we couldn't afford proper meals, we lived on *baguettes* and *parisiennes*.

But bread has a way of intimidating. When we first started giving dinner parties, along with the homemade pâtés and casseroles I would proudly serve my homemade bread. What solid worthy stuff it was too! And how long it had taken me to make. I followed carefully the very best recipes. I'd anxiously watch the yeast to make sure it was working. I'd knead and knead until my wrists ached. Then I'd wait around for the prescribed one and a half hours for it to rise, knock it back, shape it into loaves, let it prove and finally bake it. It was rarely worth all the effort. Guests would be very polite about it and impressed that I'd made it myself, but I gave up making bread. For some years after that our dinner parties were breadless. We made a virtue of not eating it. But I missed it. Until one day quite recently, I made some bread rolls almost by accident. I had wanted to make some tiny pizzas as appetisers, and not having a recipe, almost literally threw together what I thought to be the correct ingredients – yeast dissolved in a little lukewarm milk and water with a spot of sugar (I wasn't sure why, but I remembered that it was somehow necessary), more water, flour and a drop of olive oil – put it all in the food processor for a few seconds. By the time I'd made the pizzas I still seemed to have a lot of dough left which I shaped into miniature plaits, left to one side while I finished preparations for dinner. They were quite delicious. The next day I had another go to make sure it wasn't a fluke and also to make a note of quantities. And, as before, I let the dough work around *my* timetable and not vice versa. It worked. Here is the recipe and the method I used. The other 'secret' is to make it in manageable quantities. You can, of course, substitute fresh yeast for dried yeast but it isn't always available. I find the new, fast-action yeasts produce a bland, uninteresting bread.

For 8 small bread rolls or one plaited loaf

½ lb / 225 g strong white flour
¼ pint / 150 ml tepid milk and
   water mixed
pinch of sugar
1 heaped teaspoon dried yeast

1 tablespoon olive oil,
   sunflower oil or melted
   butter
½ teaspoon salt

Put all the liquid and the sugar in a basin. Sprinkle on the dried yeast and let it work and dissolve. This takes 10–15 minutes. (I have left it much longer than this while I went out shopping.)

Put the flour, salt, oil and yeasty liquid into the food processor. Process for one minute, in short bursts.

Knead together into a ball on a floured board until it is no longer sticky but elastic and smooth. Lightly oil a bowl and place the dough in it. Cover it with cling film or a damp warm teatowel and put to one side to let it rise. In a warm place it will take an hour, but if you have other things to do, leave it in a cool place and let it look after itself – for the day, or overnight. When you are ready to use it, knock the dough back, that is to say, give it a few vigorous thumps which will deflate it considerably. Then divide it and shape it as you wish. Small round rolls, finger rolls, one single small loaf or plait. Place on a greased baking tray and set aside to rise (prove) a second time. Forty minutes in a warmish kitchen should be enough. Bake near the top of a pre-heated medium hot oven (gas mark 3–4, 175°C / 350°F) for 15–20 minutes.

For me, the most convenient way to bake is to prepare the yeast first thing in the morning while I make the coffee. After breakfast mix it into the flour and leave to rise, quite often all day. About an hour before dinner, knock it back, shape and let it prove, then put it in the oven and you have warm fresh bread rolls for dinner.

I have now begun to experiment with this basic mixture. I have doubled the quantities and no harm has been done. Mixing a little wholemeal flour with the white changes the character and retains a good texture. I have also made some sweet breakfast rolls with the basic dough after its first rising. Roll it into small individual squares. Take a piece of marzipan (or ground almonds mixed with sugar and melted butter) roll this into a sausage shape and place diagonally on the square of dough. Sprinkle with cinnamon, nutmeg or mixed spices. Fold one side of the dough over the marzipan so you have a filled triangle. Then roll up from the long side, rather like making a croissant. Leave to prove and bake in the usual way.

I am now ready to experiment with herb rolls, adding fresh or dried dill weed; other good flavours would be chopped nuts, poppy seeds and raisins, grated Parmesan with paprika and, one I've tasted only recently, tomato. It produced a lovely moist dough, pale orange and tasting definitely tomatoey. About one teaspoon of purée added to the basic mixture with only one teaspoon of olive oil should work.

The possibilities really are endless, are they not? I wish I could write with as much optimism about pastry making. I cannot. I have hot hands, so am only good at making choux pastry, untouched by human hand.

WINTER

When winter comes, rather than mourn the absence of those things you have enjoyed in the previous seasons – the salads, the soft fruits, the wild mushrooms – look forward to those things which are truly at their best at this time.

Homegrown celery needs plenty of hearty frosts to give it flavour and texture. Instead of courgettes, peas and fine beans, look rather to the variety to be found amongst the cabbage family. Leaves of either the Savoy or the white cabbage stuffed with a mixture of pork and veal makes *golubtsys*, a dish made in many forms in eastern Europe. My mother-in-law, who has Russian antecedents, always makes a big pan-ful of these tasty stuffed cabbage rolls (known as pigs in blankets in Western Pennsylvania) if she knows we're coming. I sit down thinking I'll eat one or two and finish up eating four or five. Red cabbage, shredded and cooked slowly in an earthenware pot with vinegar, brown sugar and an apple is as good with roast pheasant as it is with pork casserole. Cabbage is rarely an elegant dish, largely because of its coarse, pervasive smell, but recently I devised one that was fine enough to go with calves' sweetbreads – cabbage with lavender vinegar – of which more later.

Amongst other winter goodies forced rhubarb, delicate pink and tart, makes good fresh-tasting pies. Shellfish is at its peak, as is much other fish. However, winter storms may mean that there is less of it around, so it could be more expensive than usual. After Christmas much of the game is cheaper – it is older, therefore tougher, and so the price comes down enough for you to consider it for casseroles instead of beef or pork.

Winter is a good time for the more filling, comforting dishes: big soups, dishes using beans such as cassoulet or chili con carne, crusty pies, or even suet pastry for, perhaps, a venison pudding. At the same time, you will want to serve light dishes – crisp winter salads, lightly cooked shellfish, fresh fruit. There are few finer ways to finish a winter meal than with slices of chilled tropical fruit sprinkled with a sweet wine – a Barsac or a Muscat de Beaumes de Venise.

These winter recipes will give you some ideas for simple family meals and for some grander affairs for friends. Instead of using the starters or puddings I've suggested, you may prefer to use something from the spring or autumn recipes. It will to some extent depend on what you have available, whether it's a mild or a cold winter, and on the amount of time you have.

ONIONS IN RED WINE
LAMB PAPRIKA
MARZIPAN APPLES

This is a good weekday meal especially if you have a slow cooker or a timing device on your oven. With careful planning, your meal could be ready when you come home from work. It is also a cheap meal. Because the lamb is cooked very slowly, you can use the cheapest cuts such as middle neck or scrag end.

With this meal I would serve a fairly robust red wine, perhaps the same one I used to cook the onions in. As I write this, we are still enjoying the 1982 lesser Rhône wines. The Georges Duboeuf Côte du Rhône 1982 has seen us through many meals of this kind.

I have not tried it, but if one were to dress up the casserole with dill, sour cream and noodles, I have the feeling that an Austrian white wine (a Grüner Veltliner or a Riesling) would not be inappropriate.

Onions in red wine
SERVES 4

For this I would want, if possible, to cook small onions. Otherwise the appearance of the finished dish could remind you too much of the baked apple to follow.

16–20 small onions or 4 medium-sized onions	Salt, pepper
7 fl oz / 200 ml red wine	2 teaspoons brown sugar
3 tablespoons olive oil or a mixture of oil and butter	Herbs – a pinch of thyme or rosemary
	Chopped parsley

Butter an ovenproof dish. Put half the olive oil in a frying pan, heat and cook the peeled whole onions for a few minutes until lightly golden all over. Add the sugar and stir till melted. Remove the onions and put them in the ovenproof dish. Deglaze the pan with the wine and pour it on to the onions. Season with salt, pepper and herbs. Sprinkle the remaining oil over the top of the onions. Cover with lid or foil and bake in a low oven gas mark 3, 170°C/325°F, for 40 minutes to 1 hour depending on the size of the onions.

To serve, bring the oven dish to the table, the onions sprinkled with parsley and basted with their juice, along with some crusty bread.

Lamb paprika
SERVES 4–5

3 lb/1.25 kg lamb on the bone – scrag end or middle neck, chopped for casseroling
or
1½ lb/600 g boned lamb chunks
1 medium onion, sliced
2 cloves garlic, crushed

2 sticks celery, sliced
1 tablespoon sunflower or olive oil
1 oz/25 g seasoned flour – flour mixed with salt and pepper
½ oz/15 g paprika
½ pint/300 ml stock or wine and water

Put the seasoned flour in a brown paper bag and shake in it a few pieces of lamb at a time. I find this is the best method for coating meat with flour. Put the floured pieces to one side. Carry on until all have been coated. Heat the oil in a heavy casserole or frying pan. When smoking, sear a few pieces of meat at a time until well browned. Put the pieces to one side, or transfer to a casserole. Lightly fry the onion and celery in the remaining oil until they take colour. Add to the meat. Add the paprika to the cooking pan, stir in and scrape up the residues, deglaze with the stock or mixed wine and water. Bring it to the boil and reduce slightly. Pour over the meat and add the crushed garlic. (I prefer to add my garlic raw rather than fry with the other vegetables and risk burning it, which makes it quite bitter.)

Put the casserole near the bottom of a low oven gas mark 2, 150°C/300°F, for 2½ hours or so, or in a medium oven gas mark 4, 180°C/350°F, for about 1½ hours.

This is quite a filling dish and since you will also be having a hot pudding I would suggest a crisp winter salad: some white cabbage or Chinese leaves, shredded with carrots, some fennel or celery, a few walnuts tossed in a mustardy dressing.

On the other hand, if you can't do without potatoes, and since you will have had the oven on anyway, you could bake some in their jackets alongside the casserole of lamb.

Or you could turn the dish into something like a goulash by adding a few dill seeds to the casserole. Serve it with a few spoonfuls of sour cream, and a dish of buttered noodles.

Marzipan *apples*
SERVES 4

Although Bramleys are recommended for baking, I like to use dessert apples, particularly Russets or Cox's.

If you do not want to make your own almond paste you may be able to find the Danish brand, in a sausage shape, which I find very good. It is pliable and almondy, unlike some of the hard, dry bricks sold as marzipan.

4 medium-sized apples   Cinnamon
1 oz / 25 g butter
3 oz / 75 g almond paste (see p. 19)

Core the apples. Butter four individual dishes or a baking sheet. Divide the almond paste into four. Roll each piece into a thin cork-like shape and push into the apple in place of the core. Rub the apples with a little more butter and dust with cinnamon. Bake for 30 minutes or so in a medium oven gas mark 4, 175°C / 350°F. Dessert apples will cook more quickly than cooking apples. If you put them in just before you sit down to dinner, they should be ready by the time you've reached the last course.

These are good served on their own, but you might like to serve single cream with them.

CUCUMBER AND GARLIC
CASSOULET
CHEESE
DATE, ORANGE AND WALNUT SALAD

A cool, crunchy starter is the right thing to serve before a robust dish like a cassoulet. I call it cassoulet but I doubt whether my version would find favour with the inhabitants of Toulouse where I first tasted it. On the other hand, the cassoulet of Toulouse does not necessarily find favour with the inhabitants of Carcassonne, and that of Carcassonne with the people of Castelnaudary who claim to have invented the dish in the Middle Ages.

You could hardly do better than serve a local wine with this, a Saint Chinian, a Coteaux du Tricastin or a *vin de pays de l'Hérault*.

1 cucumber	4 tablespoons yoghurt	*Cucumber and*
Salt	Fresh herbs	*garlic*
2 cloves of garlic		SERVES 4–5

Slice the cucumber very thinly – a mandolin or a food processor is invaluable. Sprinkle with salt and leave to drain for a couple of hours. Rinse and dry very thoroughly, pressing between paper towels. Crush the garlic and mix with the yoghurt and whatever chopped fresh herbs you have available. Add the cucumber and stir into the dressing. Serve with warm bread rolls.

Cassoulet
SERVES 4

I find this an ideal dish to do if I have bought ducks for a duck breast recipe. I would use two or three legs in the cassoulet and make rillettes with the rest for another day (see below). A rich, meaty sausage, such as *saucisson de Toulouse*, is ideal for cassoulet. English sausage tends to be too soft and stodgy, whereas continental-style sausages are filled with more coarsely ground meat and are better suited to long cooking. If you want to make the cassoulet for more people, increase the pieces of meat accordingly and add 2 oz / 50 g beans per person.

2 duck legs	½ pint / 300 ml duck or other
4 best end of lamb chops	stock
¾ lb / 350 g spicy sausage	½ lb / 225 g tomatoes
2 onions, sliced	Seasoning
1 stick celery, sliced	2 bay leaves
Garlic – optional	2 oz / 50 g breadcrumbs
12 oz / 350 g cannellini beans	

Soak the beans overnight. Trim any excess fat off the meat. Chop the duck legs in half. Lightly fry the meat in a non-stick frying pan to seal it and brown it all over. Remove and put to one side. Fry the onion, celery and garlic gently without letting them brown, and place in the bottom of a Dutch oven or other deep pot. Next place a layer of soaked beans. Season lightly. Add the lamb chops next and cover with more beans. Lay the duck pieces on top and cover with more beans. Finally place the sausages in the pot. Add the chopped tomatoes and the bay leaves, pour on the stock and put in the pre-heated oven for 2 hours at gas mark 2, 150°C / 300°F. Remove from the oven. Stir and sprinkle the breadcrumbs on top. Return to the oven and bake for another 20 minutes or so. Serve straight from the pot.

Follow this with some cheese perhaps and a simple salad of orange slices with chopped fresh dates and fresh walnuts.

Duck Rillettes – for another day

4 oz / 125 g belly pork	Salt
Duck legs	Pepper
Extra duck skin with plenty of	Bay leaf
fat on it, plus any more fat	Sage
from the cavity	Nutmeg

Slice the belly pork and put it in a heavy casserole. Chop the duck legs into two or three pieces and put them and the duck skin in the casserole. Season lightly and add the bay leaf. Cook at the bottom of a very low oven until all the fat has melted and the meat is cooked. This can take 3 or 4 hours. Remove from the oven. Place a sieve over a pudding basin. Remove the bones and skin from the casserole and ladle some of the remaining meat and fat into the sieve. The next process is somewhat time consuming but produces a better end result than the food processor.

Take a fork in each hand and literally pull the meat apart. It should all finish up in shreds. Pack loosely into a kilner jar or other pot adding a little melted fat. Continue until all the meat has been shredded and potted and all the fat poured around it. Make sure the top is sealed with fat. Cool, cover and then store in the refrigerator. Serve with plenty of warm bread and perhaps a pickle or two.

This recipe can be used for pork alone, rabbit or goose.

MUSHROOM SALAD
PIGS IN BLANKETS
CRANBERRY KISSEL

A deliciously warming meal, which will cook itself if you are out during the day. The starter takes only a few minutes to prepare and you can make it, and the *kissel*, the evening before. The *golubtsys* are always a very welcome smell at my mother-in-law's, Sophie Elizabeth (who will only be known as Edith), after a bitterly cold winter day spent tramping round the streets of Pittsburgh. Traditionally Sophie Elizabeth serves this with creamy mashed potatoes and sweet pickles. And to drink, a very good, local Pittsburgh beer, *Iron City*, or *Rolling Rock*, another fine Western Pennsylvania beer.

Mushroom salad
SERVES 4–6

1 lb / 450 g button or cup mushrooms
4 tablespoons olive oil
2 tablespoons red or white wine
Thinly peeled rind of half a lemon, lime or orange
½ teaspoon coriander seeds
1 small onion

There seem to exist two schools of thought about mushroom salad – one for cooking them, one for leaving them raw. Sometimes I follow one, sometimes the other. Let us cook this one. Wipe and slice the mushrooms. Heat half the olive oil in a frying pan and quickly stir fry the mushrooms; no more than a minute at most. Remove from the heat and transfer to a flat serving dish. Blend the rest of the oil with wine and pour it over the hot mushrooms. Add the lemon peel and the coriander. Stir in. Thinly slice the onion and add to the mushroom mixture. Allow to cool, chill and serve with brown bread and butter. The hot mushrooms absorb the flavour of the wine and olive oil and give off their own juices to form a delicious dressing.

Pigs in blankets
SERVES 4–6

These are very good heated up the following day – should you have any left over.

1 head of cabbage
8 oz / 225 g minced pork
8 oz / 225 g minced veal
8 oz / 225 g minced beef
2 oz / 50 g soft white breadcrumbs
1 teaspoon dill seeds
2 onions
2 cloves garlic
½ pint / 300 ml dry cider
Small tin of tomatoes or ½ lb / 225 g fresh ripe tomatoes
1 teaspoon juniper berries
Seasoning
Chopped chives
Sour cream or smatana

Carefully separate the cabbage leaves, discarding any bruised or rotten ones. Chop the cabbage heart and reserve. Trim away the woody base of each leaf and cut out the central stem if it is very tough.

Mix together the three meats, breadcrumbs and dill seed. Chop the onions and one clove of garlic and add these plus a little seasoning. Drop the cabbage leaves a few at a time into a large pan of boiling salted water to soften them. Remove, rinse and drain.

Take a handful of stuffing and place it on a cabbage leaf, overlapping it in the centre if you have removed the rib. Roll up, tucking the ends in as you roll. Continue until you have used up all the cabbage leaves and the stuffing. Lightly grease a deepish ovenproof dish and lay the chopped cabbage over the base. Arrange the stuffed cabbage rolls on top, the loose ends underneath. Boil up the cider with the chopped tomatoes, juniper berries and the remaining clove of garlic. Reduce a little and pour over the cabbage. Cover and cook in a very low oven for a very long time or towards the bottom of a warm oven gas mark 3, 170°C/325°F, for 2½–3 hours.

Serve with a spoonful of soured cream and sprinkle with chopped chives.

Cranberry kissel

SERVES 4

These tangy little red berries are too often relegated to sauces and jellies to serve with meat. They make delicious sorbet or ice cream. This is a traditional Russian dessert.

1 lb / 450 g cranberries
1 pint / 600 ml water
4–6 oz / 125–175 g sugar – to taste

2 tablespoons potato starch or cornflour

Wash the berries and simmer until very soft in a pint of water. Sieve the pulp. Stir the sugar into the brightly coloured juice. Heat until melted. Mix the potato starch with two tablespoons cold water. Stir into the syrup and, continuing to stir, bring it to the boil when you will see the mixture thicken. Boil for no more than two minutes to cook the starch, any longer and the kissel will begin to thin. Pour into a glass bowl. Cool and chill. Serve with thin cream, thick cream, yoghurt, cream cheese, or plain.

RAW FISH SALAD
POT ROAST PARTRIDGES
GRATIN OF POTATOES AND MUSHROOMS
BAKED PEARS WITH ROQUEFORT

Should you want to celebrate all twelve days of Christmas, here is a meal to go with the partridge and the pear tree on the first day, Christmas Eve. We would treat ourselves to the best champagne we could afford, and then we would open one of our special clarets. To finish, a Sauternes almost certainly, perhaps our 1976 Château Suduiraut.

Raw fish salad
SERVES 6

What makes this salad different is that the fish is served raw. It was quite a revelation to me the first time I ever tasted raw fish. It was delicious and now I often serve this. The secret is to slice the fish quite thinly, keep the ingredients separate on the plate and arrange as attractively as possible, not in a mish-mash. The preparation bears some relation to *gravad lax* but does not need as long to marinate. I normally use three or four of the following: salmon, salmon trout, monkfish, sole, turbot, scallops or fresh mackerel fillet. Because you can't ask even the kindliest fishmonger for 3 oz of salmon etc. I usually buy half a pound of each, or a fillet (in the case of mackerel) and use what is left over for fish soup or fish florentine, see p. 25. You will, I am sure, have asked your fishmonger for bones and scraps, for soup or stock for future use.

2 measures of vodka	Dash of cayenne pepper
Sea salt	12 oz / 350 g fish
Pepper (black or white)	Garnish
Juice of half a lime	

Combine the first five ingredients in a china bowl, ignoring the fact that it has the makings of a fearsome cocktail. This is the marinade.

Trim the fish and slice as neatly as possible, using your sharpest knife (you will find that you have quite a lot of scraps and pieces left over). The way you slice will depend on the cut of fish you buy; except for scallops which you can easily cut horizontally into two rounds, I slice the fish vertically as if into mini-steaks rather than into long slices along the length of the fillet. Each serving should contain three or four neat slices of each fish you use. When you have achieved these neat slices, put into the marinade and leave for between 30 minutes to two hours in the refrigerator, turning occasionally.

To serve, arrange in a decorative fashion, and in a single layer on individual plates. For garnish I would use something to contrast with the pale pink or white of the fish, but only a very small sprig, you don't want to swamp the plate. At the moment I am using pickled samphire which I made last summer. (See p. 146.) When it runs out I shall use chervil, parsley, fresh dill or a few fronds of fennel. A sliced *cornichon* would accompany the fish quite well provided it was not too strongly pickled.

Hand pumpernickel or brown bread separately.

Pot roast
partridges
SERVES 4

4 prepared partridges	Tablespoon brandy
2 oz / 50 g butter	Small glass of port or
1 tablespoon finely chopped	vermouth or red wine
fresh herbs	Bramble jelly
Salt and pepper	

Mix the herbs, seasoning and butter. Smear some over the birds and put the rest inside the cavity. Heat a little more butter in a large casserole and sear the birds all over. Pour on the brandy and set alight. Add the port. Cover with a lid or foil and place in the oven pre-heated to gas mark 5, 190°C / 375°F. Cook for 35 minutes. Test for doneness. Drain off all the cooking juices into a small saucepan. Add a teaspoon of wild blackberry jelly and reduce until becoming syrupy.

Serve the partridges on small rounds of toast on individual serving plates with a spoonful or two of sauce. Accompanying vegetables should be green and crisp – broccoli, mangetout, celery sticks etc. Hand some more bramble jelly separately. In addition, a gratin of potatoes and mushrooms will be very welcome. (See p. 89.)

Baked pears
with Roquefort
SERVES 4

4 good ripe pears	½ oz / 15 g butter
2 oz / 50 g Roquefort or blue	Cinnamon or nutmeg
Stilton	

Peel the pears. Cut in half and scoop out the core, enlarging the cavity slightly. Crumble the cheese and mix with most of the butter. Use the rest to butter four individual ovenproof dishes. Spoon the cheese into the cavity in the pears and sandwich the two halves together again. Place in the dishes, sprinkle with cinnamon or nutmeg and bake for 15 to 20 minutes at gas mark 4, 180°C / 350°F, covered with buttered paper. Serve warm.

MOULES MARINIÈRE
GAME PIE
CABBAGE WITH LAVENDER VINEGAR
GRILLED GOAT'S CHEESE
TROPICAL FRUITS

As long as the weather is cold you can be sure of getting good shellfish. *Moules marinière* is one of the dishes we look forward to in the winter and we'll often make a whole meal of it. But I serve mussels for dinner parties too – either in individual bowls or in a large white tureen with a china ladle.

Not all game is suitable for roasting and if you are unsure of its age it is probably wisest to casserole it. I like to cook a mixture of game and serve it under a crisp crust. That is, I did until I tasted a novel way of doing it at Hilaire, South Kensington, where Simon Hopkinson is the chef. The traditional English crumble topping was transferred from the pudding trolley to the main course and it worked very well.

A red Portuguese wine, a Dão as old as you can get, would be fine with the game pie.

Moules marinière
SERVES 4–5

4 lb / 1.85 kg mussels – when did they stop selling them by the quart?
2 shallots or small onions
1 stick of celery – optional, not traditional, but adds a good flavour
1 glass of dry white wine
2 tablespoons fine, soft, white breadcrumbs
2 tablespoons chopped parsley
White pepper
Knob of butter – optional

Scrub the mussels under cold water, discarding any that remain open. Tug off the beard wedged in the straight side of the shell and knock off any barnacles. Rinse thoroughly and drain. Put the mussels in a pan. Chop the shallots and celery very finely and add to the pan. Pour on the glass of wine. Cover with a tightly fitting lid and raise the heat to the fullest. Steam the mussels, shaking the pan a few times. Peep in after two minutes. Most of the mussels should be open. Toss in the breadcrumbs and parsley, sprinkle with pepper and add the butter if you are using it. Replace the lid for another thirty seconds. Shake the pan vigorously to coat all the mussels with parsley and breadcrumbs.

Serve in a large tureen or in individual soup bowls, with plenty of bread and a soupspoon.

A variation on this recipe is *moules poulette*. When the mussels are cooked, remove a ladleful of juice from the pan. Beat in ¼ pint / 150 ml double cream and 1 egg yolk. Return to the pan and let it heat through but without allowing it to come near the boil.

Game pie
SERVES 4

For this recipe you can use any or all of the following: venison, hare, pheasant, wild rabbit, pigeon. Explain to your butcher what you are preparing so that he can give you cuts suitable for casseroling.

1½ lb / 675 g game off the bone	¼ pint / 150 ml stock
1 glass port or red wine	Seasoning
1 tablespoon oil	2 cloves garlic
1 carrot	5 oz / 150 g plain flour
1 onion	3 oz / 75 g butter
1 stick celery	
½ oz / 15 g dried wild mushrooms or failing these, 4 oz / 125 g fresh mushrooms	

Cut the meat into small chunks. Heat the oil and gently fry the sliced carrot, onion and celery until they begin to brown. Pour on the wine and then remove from the heat. Cool the marinade and then pour it over the meat. Leave overnight, or for at least a few hours. If using dried mushrooms, soak them in a bowl of warm water until plumped out and soft. Drain and dry the meat. Strain the marinade and set it aside. When I have leftover marinade vegetables I usually try and add them to some soup or stock so as not to waste them.

Heat a non-stick frying pan. Taking a few pieces at a time, sear the meat all over and transfer it to a casserole. Pour the stock and the marinade into the frying pan and boil, scraping up any residue (with a wooden spoon). Pour over the meat. Add the drained, sliced mushrooms. Season lightly and add the crushed garlic. Cover and cook in the oven at gas mark 2–3, 150–170°C/300–325°F, for 1½–2 hours. You can prepare the dish to this stage the day before. Like most casseroles, it benefits from the blending of flavours overnight.

For the final preparation transfer the meat to a shallow dish, leaving at least ½ in/1 cm for the topping.

Rub the butter into the flour until it resembles fine breadcrumbs. Spoon evenly over the meat and press down a little. Bake in a hot oven gas mark 6–7, 200–220°C/400–425°F, for 15–20 minutes.

Crisp vegetables are best with this rather than purées, so I would serve a dish of cabbage prepared with lavender vinegar, which raises an ordinary vegetable to something rather special.

I have made a version of lavender vinegar by steeping fresh lavender buds in cider or white wine vinegar and standing this in a sunny spot for as long as possible. Otherwise I buy Lavender Dessert Vinegar made at Hulbrook House Herb Farm in Surrey.

Cabbage with lavender vinegar
SERVES 4–5

1 lb/450 g white cabbage
2 oz/50 g butter
1 tablespoon brown sugar

1–2 tablespoons lavender vinegar

Shred the cabbage finely. Heat the butter in a heavy frying pan or wok. Adding a drop of oil will stop it burning and I would add sesame oil, as I like the flavour. Stir the cabbage in the butter and after a minute or so add the brown sugar. Cook a little longer and then add the vinegar. Raise the heat and stir vigorously for 20 seconds or so. Serve the cabbage still slightly crunchy with the pan juices poured over.

The lavender somehow gets rid of the sulphurous, cabbagey smell which can be so off-putting and it adds a fine flavour of its own, so the essential quality of the cabbage is still there but enhanced. Coleslaw with lavender vinegar in the dressing further demonstrates how well the two things go together.

For a dinner party I would probably follow this with some grilled goat's cheese on toast accompanied by its own salad. And to finish, a platter of tropical fruits, sliced and piled up, possibly sprinkled with sweet white wine, possibly not. A squeeze of fresh lime might be even nicer, particularly if you can get papaya (paw paw) and mango.

Grilled goat's cheese To prepare the goat's cheese you will need 3½–4 oz / 85–100 g of fresh white goat's cheese – usually French, but occasionally now made in England. What you will *not* want to use is Gjetost, Norwegian goat's cheese which, when toasted, is indistinguishable from hot, melted fudge. Toast 4 slices of bread on one side only. Slice the cheese. Lightly butter the untoasted side of the bread and lay the cheese on top. Put under a hot grill for about 3 minutes until melted and bubbling nicely. Serve hot with a very few leaves of the most exotic salad you can find – oak leaf lettuce, endive, chicory, radicchio, watercress – dressed simply with a little olive oil and lemon juice.

BAKED MUSSELS
ROAST FILLET OF BEEF
BAKED MUSHROOMS & SALAD
APRICOTS IN WINE

This is an expensive meal but one which can be prepared in a very short time, provided you are able to marinate the beef the day before and the apricots preferably several days before.

My mother served us this meal one Friday evening after she, and we, had had a long, busy week. It was something that took her little time to put together but was a most elegant and delicious dinner.

Serve a young Muscadet or Sauvignon-de-Saint-Bris with the first course. The crispness of the wine will perfectly complement the mussels. With the beef we would probably serve a good 1976 claret, perhaps the Château Branaire-Ducru which we have been enjoying over the last couple of years. Or a 1966, if we really wanted a treat for ourselves and our guests, a Château Magdelaine or a Château Palmer.

Baked mussels This method of cooking shellfish is much used in Nantes and is
SERVES 4 particularly good with mussels, although traditionally a preparation for scallops.

3 dozen medium-sized mussels   Parsley
4 oz / 100 g butter   Pepper
4 oz / 100 g soft white
   breadcrumbs

Wash, scrub and trim the mussels. Steam open and remove the fish from their shells. Divide the butter between four small ramekins and smear it thickly all over. Then line each ramekin with breadcrumbs and divide the mussels among the ramekins. Cover with any remaining breadcrumbs. Sprinkle with a little pepper. Bake at the top of a very hot oven for 5–7 minutes. Serve sprinkled with parsley.

Roast fillet of beef
SERVES 4–5

1½ lb / 700 g beef fillet in a piece
⅓ bottle claret
2 tablespoons olive oil
1 sliced onion
1 chopped carrot
1 chopped stick of celery
4 cloves crushed garlic
Salt and pepper

Trim the fillet of any fat, membrane and gristle. Mix the wine, olive oil, garlic and vegetables and pour over the meat. Leave overnight.

Pre-heat the oven to gas mark 7, 220°C / 425°F. Remove the meat from the marinade and dry it thoroughly on paper towels. Heat a non-stick frying pan and sear the meat all over. Transfer to a wire rack in a roasting pan. Place in the oven and roast for 20–30 minutes, depending on how pink you like it. Remove from the oven and keep in a warm place while you prepare the sauce, which is simply a reduction of the marinade to which you add the cooking juices. If you want a more elaborate sauce, you can add herbs, brandy or port, cream or butter etc.

Serve the fillet whole on a long platter surrounded by watercress and carve it at table. Baked mushrooms and green salad are the perfect accompaniment.

Apricots in wine
SERVES 6–8

This dish is not worth preparing unless you use good quality apricots and a wine of the quality you would drink.

1 lb dried apricots   1 bottle Sauternes or Barsac

Wash and dry the apricots. Pack into a one kilo glass preserving jar and fill to the top with wine. Leave for at least 48 hours, better still a week. Shake occasionally. You will notice how the apricots plump out and absorb the wine. Serve a few for each guest in a wine glass with a little of the juice, or let people spear their own from the jar.

A jar of apricots prepared in this way and suitably labelled, makes an excellent gift. I have kept some of mine for about three months.

WARM QUAIL EGGS AND LEEK SALAD
ARTICHOKE RISOTTO
PRUNE ICE CREAM

Because no fish or meat is used in this meal it is something that you could serve to vegetarians. If you do, make sure that you use vegetable stock for the risotto. (See p. 62)

Ask your wine merchant to recommend you a Chianti riserva, preferably one in a Bordeaux bottle, not a straw-covered flask.

Warm quail eggs and leek salad
SERVES 4

Radicchio and curly endive look particularly good in this dish. Walnut oil and sherry vinegar would make the best base for the dressing.

3 leeks	Salad 'greens'
1 dozen quail eggs	A few chopped walnuts
1 tablespoon double cream, yoghurt or *fromage frais*	Dressing

Quail eggs are difficult to cook just right so that the white is set and the yolks not quite. This way works for me. Put the eggs in a pan of cold water. Bring to the boil and simmer while you count to 30. Remove to the sink and hold the pan under running cold water. Stop when the water in the pan is no longer hot, just warm. The reason for this is that you are serving a warm salad and need to maintain the eggs at a certain temperature. Wash and shred the leeks lengthwise into 3 in / 7.5 cm strips. Drop into boiling water and simmer until tender. Drain and return to the pan with cream or yoghurt, etc. Stir well in and keep them warm. Arrange the leaves on individual serving plates. Shell the eggs and return them to the warm water.

On each plate make a nest of leeks holding three quail eggs. Pour over the dressing. Scatter on the walnuts.

A non-vegetarian version of this would be to serve in addition gently fried quail breasts sliced on to the salad.

Artichoke risotto
SERVES 4 AS A
MAIN COURSE,
6 AS A STARTER

The first time I tasted this was in Prospero's, one of the many excellent restaurants in Milan. It preceded a plate of the most perfectly, simply cooked calves' liver which, in other circumstances, would have been the highlight of the meal. This risotto was rich and creamy, though no cream went into its making I'm sure, with that most distinct particular taste of artichoke. I couldn't wait to get home and experiment with the dish myself. It is wonderfully soothing as a supper dish, and warming on a cold night. Artichokes can be expensive in winter but this is an economical way of using them – three being enough for four people. The best rice for risotto is *cristallo* or *arborio*. Really, nothing else will do.

3 globe artichokes (or 2 if huge)

2 pints / 1 litre stock (see following recipe)

10½ oz / 300 g rice

2 shallots or 1 medium onion, finely chopped

2 oz / 50 g butter

2 tablespoons olive oil

First prepare the artichokes. Snap off the outer leaves. The 'snap' will come about two-thirds or three-quarters of the way down the leaf. This will remove the stringy part of the leaf and leave the fleshy base. Slice the top off the artichoke, about an inch from the bottom. This is, of course, all relative to the size of the artichoke. The fleshy part of the vegetable is the base, and the part that you eat. Young artichokes have tender fleshy leaves so that you need to remove less. Older vegetables are more stringy so you need to remove more. If the stalk has not already been cut off in the greengrocer's remove it by twisting it off as close to the base as possible. This will remove some of the fibres. Now, with a pointed spoon and/or sharp knife, remove the 'choke', the hairy centre of the artichoke, and the tiny leaves which surround it. When you have finished you should be left with the base of the artichoke surrounded by stubby cut-off leaves. Slice finely and leave in a bowl of water to which you have added a drop of vinegar or lemon juice to stop the artichoke discolouring.

Melt all the oil and half the butter in a heavy pan or casserole. Cook the shallots or onion until turning soft and transparent. Add the drained artichoke. Meanwhile heat the stock. Stir the rice with the artichokes and onion or shallots until glistening with oil, taking care not to burn the rice. Turn up the heat. Add ¼ pint / 150 ml of the heated stock and stir. When this is almost absorbed add a further ¼ pint / 150 ml of stock and let it absorb. Stir the mixture fairly continuously. Cooking risotto is quite a different discipline to producing the fluffy, separate grains of rice in a pilaff. Then the rice is not stirred and is cooked undisturbed with all the liquid added, at once, at the beginning. You must watch a risotto all the time. It is not something that can be left and come back to. The dish will probably take about 30–35 minutes once you have added the first batch of stock. The stock should be added in relatively small quantities, and each absorbed before more is added. By the time you only have a $\frac{1}{4}$ pint / 150 ml left, the rice will be almost cooked, creamy all the way through, and the artichokes will be tender. You may not need to add the remaining stock, but stir in what is left of the butter and serve immediately.

This is a versatile dish: the method can be used for other kinds of risotto, substituting your chosen ingredients for the artichoke. Resist the temptation to use frozen artichokes – they will not do.

Vegetable stock

2 pints / 1–1½ l water	Any or all of these, as
2 tablespoons oil	available: small bunch of
3 carrots	watercress, mushroom stalks
3 onions	and peelings, parsley stalks,
3 sticks of celery	piece of fennel
2 leeks, sliced	2 oz / 50 g dried beans
2 ripe tomatoes	1 oz / 25 g lentils
	1 oz / 25 g pearl barley
	Seasoning to taste

Wash and soak the beans, lentils and barley overnight. Heat the oil in a large heavy casserole and fry the chopped carrots, onion and celery until golden brown but not burnt. Add the rest of the vegetables and turn in the oil. Pour on all the water, drain the pulses and barley and add to the pot. Bring slowly to the boil. Remove any scum from the surface and turn down the heat to maintain a steady simmer for 2–3 hours. A piece of onion skin added to the stock for the first half hour will give it a good colour. Strain and season to taste, if you are going to use the stock as a base for soup or risotto. If you are using it to make a reduction for sauces do not season to taste at this stage as the reduction concentrates the flavours and it is so easy to produce a too-salty sauce.

This is a good way of using up fruits in liqueur from Christmas time. There is a chance though, that if they are very alcoholic they may not freeze. This happened to me when I tried to make ice cream by puréeing apricots in Barsac, adding double cream and freezing. The *sorbetière* beat it beautifully but it was never going to freeze so I served instead a light, frothy, ice-cold apricot mousse with almond biscuits. This was different, but equally good.

Prune ice cream
SERVES 4–6

1 lb / 450 g soaked and softened prunes

½ pint / 300 ml double cream or equivalent of good thick yoghurt

¼ pint / 150 ml single cream, milk or buttermilk

2 oz / 50 g sugar

¼ pint / 150 ml water

1 Earl Grey tea bag

Make a purée of the prunes and cream. Freeze, and stir occasionally. Melt the sugar in the water. Bring it to the boil and infuse the teabag in it for 1½ minutes. Remove. Reduce the mixture until it becomes syrupy. Cool. Chill and serve poured over the ice-cream – or mousse, if you have soaked your prunes in Armagnac.

BOUDIN DE FRUITS DE MER
NOISETTES OF VENISON
GREEN SALAD WITH HERBS
JEWEL BOX

Here is a menu for a dinner party when you have plenty of preparation time. It is *not* a good idea to leave the stuffing of the seafood sausages until half an hour before your guests are due. The meal itself does not take long to cook and you can do most of the preparation in advance so it is a meal that might fit round your own timetable.

I would prepare the meat the night before, and the seafood sausages and the sponge base for the pudding the morning before they are to be eaten. Further preparation will involve poaching the sausages; making the sauce; preparing the vegetables to accompany the venison; the salad; the fruit for the pudding; and then, finally, grilling the seafood sausages and cooking the venison. I would do these last two not before required which will mean your leaving your guests for a short while before the meal and, again, before the main course.

With this same meal we have served a 1982 Mâcon-Lugny, i.e. a Mâcon as young as possible of a good year, followed by a 1976 Château Lynch-Bages. On another occasion, we drank an older white burgundy from a great vintage, a 1978 Chablis Premier Cru Fourchaumes, followed by a 1976 Gevrey-Chambertin. At both meals we served luscious Austrian wines with the pudding: a 1976 Donnerskirchner Sonnenberg Beerenauslese and a 1971 Ruster Trockenbeerenauslese.

Boudin de fruits de mer
SERVES 4

This is without doubt a very glamorous, effective dish. It can be as cheap or as expensive as you choose, depending on whether you use whiting or sole for the *mousseline*. It is however very time-consuming to prepare. After you have puréed the fish it must then be forced through a sieve – this can take a good half hour – but the resulting light texture of the dish is worth the effort. Filling the sausage skin is maddeningly fiddly, but once you have mastered it, the end result is very pleasing, a plate of smooth pale sausages filled with all sorts of goodies – scallops, prawns, nuggets of sole.

It is a dish that will lend itself to many combinations of fish and sauces once you are familiar with the basic principles. The recipe I give here is a relatively cheap one, the one I used when teaching myself how to make seafood sausages.

A word about sausage casings. You can of course get them from wholesale suppliers, but who wants a thousand sausage skins? I think the answer is to find yourself a butcher who makes his or her own sausages and ask if you can have enough casing for a dozen or so sausages. It keeps well for several days in a little salted water in a bowl in the refrigerator.

Remember to ask your fishmonger for the fish bones and trimmings, plus any extra he can spare.

1 lb / 450 g skinned whiting fillet in pieces	5 fl oz / 150 ml double cream or *crème fraîche*
4 scallops or ¼ lb / 125 g peeled prawns	Up to ¼ pint / 150 ml fish stock Salt, white pepper
2 egg whites	Sausage casing
1 egg yolk	

Make ¾ pint / 400 ml fish stock with the bones and trimmings. Trim, clean and prepare the scallops in the usual way. Remove the coral and set aside. Slice three scallops into two or three rounds. Reserve eight of these. Chop the rest, with the remaining scallop, into tiny cubes. Put the whiting, with the scallop coral, eggs, cream and five tablespoons of stock into a blender or food processor. Process until a smooth purée is obtained.

If you are substituting prawns for the scallops, divide into three portions; keep one portion for garnish, chop one portion into tiny chunks, process the rest with the whiting.

Work a small amount at a time through a sieve, adding a little more stock if necessary to help the mixture through. When it has all been sieved, season to taste. Stir in the chopped scallops or prawns.

Rinse the casing and cut off 10–12 in / 25–30 cm length, knot about an inch or so from one end. Open the other end of the casing and roll it back over the first two fingers of your left hand (if you're right handed). Use a small coffeespoon or mustardspoon for scooping up the mixture and forcing it into the casing. A sausage-making attachment would no doubt do the job in a trice! By hand it is laborious and fairly messy, but to my mind the end result is worth it. I have never tried it, but I do wonder if an icing bag might not be useful in this operation? Anyway, fill loosely for 6–8 in / 15–20 cm. The sausage will curve nicely as sausages do. Tie the other end and snip off with an inch or so spare. Continue for three more sausages.

To cook, place in a shallow pan, cover with warm water and bring slowly to simmering point. Simmer very gently for five or six minutes. Remove from the water and drain. Heat the grill. Brush the sausages with milk, cream or melted butter and put on the grill rack nearest to the heat. Keep there until the sausages begin to brown. Remove immediately. It is *not* necessary to grill them on the other side. The browning is for appearance only. The first time I made this dish (for a dinner party, which was rather a rash thing to do) I did turn the sausages over to brown on the other side. They exploded.

To serve, snip off the loose ends of the casing and the knots. Place one sausage on each plate and surround it with a pool of your favourite sauce and a few slices of sautéed scallops or prawns.

Here is a nice easy sauce recipe to serve with it. Reduce the rest of the fish stock to about six tablespoons in a shallow pan over a high flame. Add a teaspoon of brandy if you like, and/or a couple of tablespoons of the white wine you plan to serve with the fish. Reduce again and add three tablespoons of cream. Cook and stir for another 30 seconds or so to let all the flavours amalgamate, and add salt and pepper to taste.

Noisettes of venison
SERVES 4

Venison is an excellent choice for a special occasion meal, if you are lucky enough to be able to get hold of it. It is expensive, but it is such a rich, gamey meat with a concentrated flavour that you do not need to serve a very large portion. In addition, it is a lean meat and has little waste. Keep it in a winey marinade for a few days and you will then be able to make a delicious accompanying sauce.

For this dish, as in all others where wine is used in the preparation, it is important to use a decent wine, one you would be prepared to drink. A thin, acid wine will almost certainly give a sour, thin sauce.

1 lb 4 oz / 550 g loin or fillet of venison, in one piece
½ bottle of red wine
3 tablespoons port (optional)
2 cloves garlic
1 onion
1 carrot
1 stick of celery

Pinch of dried herbs or a sprig or two of fresh thyme, marjoram or rosemary
2 oz / 50 g butter
1 tablespoon olive or sunflower oil
2 teaspoons fruit jelly – redcurrant, cranberry etc. (see p. 145)
Seasoning

Trim the venison if necessary. Depending on its size and shape, slice into four or eight steaks. Put in a china or plastic bowl and pour on the wine and port. Add the herbs and chopped vegetables, cover and refrigerate for 12–72 hours, depending on your own personal taste, how fresh the meat is, and how much time you have available. I find that, generally speaking, in this country meat is not hung for as long as it should be. Once marinaded, the venison and its sauce will not take much more than 10 minutes to cook, so it can be prepared after the first course, provided you have everything ready and the venison is drained and dried.

In a heavy frying pan, large enough to take the venison steaks in one layer, heat half the butter and all the oil. When this is beginning to smoke, put in all the pieces of meat and sear for a minute or so. Reduce the heat slightly and cook for a further 3–5 minutes (depending on the thickness of the meat and how well-done you like it). Turn up the heat again and turn the steaks over. Sear for a minute, reduce the heat and cook for 2–3 minutes more, or until you judge it sufficiently cooked. Remove the venison and keep warm on a plate. Turn up the heat once more and deglaze the pan with the strained marinade, scraping up any residue. Reduce the marinade to a few spoonfuls. Add the fruit jelly. When this has melted add small quantities of the remaining butter, a little at a time, stirring continuously. The butter will amalgamate with and slightly thicken the sauce. Make sure the heat is not too high or the butter will simply melt. Season to taste. Arrange the venison on heated individual plates. Spoon a little of the sauce next to the venison and serve with a little more fruit jelly, a few steamed mangetouts or green beans and a spoonful of vegetable purée, celeriac or Jerusalem artichoke perhaps. Take care not to crowd the plate, and make sure that each item is separate and arranged as decoratively as possible.

Green salad with herbs

For this, simply choose the maximum variety of fresh green things, hard to do at this time of year, and dress it up with whatever you can find in the way of chives, parsley, watercress, even a pinch or two of fresh thyme, rosemary and snipped-up sage. Add a few walnuts or pinenuts and for the dressing use the best oil you have, plus a little lemon juice or flavoured wine vinegar.

Jewel box
SERVES 4–6

This is a rather fancy name for a very easy sponge gâteau. First bake two sponge squares or rectangles. Cut a smaller square or rectangle from one, leaving a frame. Sandwich the frame to the other sponge with a good jam or jelly and you have made a box. Fill it half full with whipped cream, flavoured if you like with liqueur, orange flower water or what you will, then fill with a few each of the best, most exotic fruits you can find – cape gooseberries, grapes, peeled lychees, figs, kumquats, segments of mandarins. Add a few walnut halves. If you can't get enough good-looking fresh fruit, use some that has been crystallised or glacé. Place the remaining piece of sponge on top, 'hinging' it with some more jam so that it looks like a half-open lid. Serve on a plate surrounded by more fruit 'jewels', if you like.

Here is my foolproof sponge recipe.

3 large eggs	4 oz / 125 g self-raising flour,
4 oz / 125 g castor sugar	sieved
	2 dessertspoons hot water

Pre-heat the oven to gas mark 7, 220°C/425°F.

Whisk together the eggs and sugar until thick, creamy and pale. If you do this in a basin set in a pan of hot water it helps stabilise the mixture. Using a metal spoon lightly fold in the sieved flour. Add the water and mix gently. Spread the mixture in two oiled cake tins. Bake towards the top of the oven for 12–15 minutes until golden brown.

Remove from oven and let the cakes cool in their tins for a minute or two. Ease them away from the tin gently with your fingers and a palette knife. Turn out on to a wire rack. Cool.

CHICKEN LIVER AND ROQUEFORT SALAD
PAPPARDELLE WITH GAME SAUCE
CARAMEL PEARS

If you have jugged a hare, casseroled some pigeons or roasted a brace of birds, try to keep some of the meat sauce to turn into a rich game sauce to serve with the broad pasta ribbons called *pappardelle*. It is one of my favourite ways of using leftovers. Alternatively, buy just one pigeon and it will give you enough meat to make the dish from scratch. I like to make my own *pappardelle*, cutting them diagonally from sheets of thin pasta dough with a fluted pastry wheel which gives the pasta a good shape.

Ask your wine supplier for a Sassicaia, an Italian wine from a small, gravelly property near Livorno made, it is said, from 100% Cabernet Sauvignon grapes. It is wonderful.

Chicken liver
& Roquefort
salad
SERVES 4

½ lb / 225 g chicken or duck's	liver	Lemon juice
¼ lb / 100 g Roquefort or other	blue cheese	Salt
Oil		Pepper
		Lettuce, radicchio, endive,
		watercress, chicory

Clean and trim the livers, carefully removing any greenish parts and the sinews. Soaking them in milk for a few hours in advance will improve their colour and flavour. Dry the livers in paper towels, slicing the larger pieces in two.

Toss your salad vegetables in the oil, salt, pepper and lemon and add chunks of the cheese. Arrange on individual plates. Put a few drops of oil in the frying pan, enough to stop the meat from sticking and, when smoking, fry all the liver for 2–3 minutes, shaking the pan a few times, not stirring as this tends to break them up. When ready – that is, still slightly pink in the middle when you stick a knife-point in – place the liver pieces on top of the salad, pour on any pan juices and serve while still warm.

Pappardelle with game sauce

SERVES 4 AS A MAIN COURSE, 6 AS A STARTER

1 lb / 450 g *pappardelle* or *tagliatelle* (see p. 25 for pasta making)

Sauce

3 oz / 75 g smoked bacon
1 onion
1 oz / 25 g raisins
1 oz / 25 g sun-dried tomatoes, chopped – optional
1 oz / 25 g ricotta
½ oz / 15 g ground almonds

½ square of dark chocolate
½ pint / 300 ml game stock
4–6 oz / 125–175 g cooked meat – hare, pheasant, pigeon, grouse etc.
Garlic, lemon zest, parsley to garnish

Cut the bacon into matchsticks and fry quickly in a heavy saucepan. When the fat begins to run, stir in the thinly sliced onion and cook until golden. Add the raisins, tomatoes and ricotta. The latter will melt and turn the sauce creamy. Then add the chocolate and almonds to thicken the mixture. Add the stock, stirring all the time to amalgamate the mixture. Cook gently until the onion and the bacon are done. Then add the shredded or chopped meat. Heat through thoroughly. Cook the pasta according to the directions, drain and tip into the serving dish. Toss with a little olive oil or butter and pour the piping hot game sauce over it. Serve immediately with a *gremolata* garnish – chopped parsley, garlic and lemon zest.

Caramel pears

SERVES 4

4 even-shaped pears
3 oz / 75 g castor sugar

3 oz / 75 g butter
¼ pint / 150 ml double cream

Peel the pears, keeping the stalks on. In a heavy pan allow the sugar to melt over a very low heat. Add the butter, then the pears. Cook slowly until the pears are soft but not breaking up. During the cooking the pears will have given off some of their juice and you will have a good buttery syrup. Remove the pears with a slotted spoon. Reduce the syrup a little and add the cream. Bring to the boil and cook for three or four minutes when it will turn a rich, warm, caramel colour. Remove from the heat. Pour over the pears and serve cold.

BEAN SOUP
GRILLED COD WITH WATERCRESS PUREE
SALAD WITH RAISINS AND WALNUTS
GRAPES AND GRAPEFRUIT

This is a warming, inexpensive meal full of good flavours. There must be as many recipes for bean soup as there are cooks who have ever prepared it; it changes according to the beans you use, the stock it is based on, what you add to it, whether you serve it smooth or chunky. It can be a starter, or a meal in itself if you add dumplings, or sausages or bacon pieces, when all you will want with it is a salad and some good, homemade, crusty bread, followed by crisp apples and the best cheese you can find. Sometimes I make bean soup from leftover cassoulet (see p. 49) but I also like to make a large pot of it from scratch. It is best cooked slowly and therefore the sort of thing you can leave cooking in a low oven or a slow cooking pot for most of the day. The meal is then quite easy to put together – soup, followed by some lightly grilled cod and, to finish, a sharp fruit salad.

A simple Bourgogne Aligoté would be a good accompaniment to this meal.

Bean soup
SERVES 4

Any dried beans can be used for the soup – haricot, cannellini, red kidney, black, navy, black-eyed etc. The variety will affect the colour, of course, but not the quality. For the garnish use finely chopped parsley, chives, watercress, grated lemon or orange zest – as you wish.

8 oz / 225 g dried beans	1 dessertspoon mustard
Knuckle of pork or bacon	½ teaspoon cumin seed
1 onion	Garlic – to taste, optional
1 stick of celery	Garnish
1 small tin of tomatoes	

Soak the beans in water overnight. Next morning rinse them, bring to the boil in fresh water and boil for 15 minutes. Then drain and rinse again. Tip them into a large heavy casserole. Wash and dry the knuckle and lay it on top of the beans. Surround with the chopped onion, celery, tomato, and garlic if you are using it. Mix the mustard with a little water, wine or stock and pour over the beans. Sprinkle on the cumin seed and cover the whole lot with water. Bring slowly to the boil, skim the surface, add ¼ pint / 150 ml more water, bring back to the boil, cover and cook on top of the stove or in a very low oven for 3–4 hours. Longer cooking will not hurt it. Remove the knuckle from the pot; by now the meat and rind will be falling off it. Fish out as much of the rind as you can. You can then return some of the meat to the soup if you wish but it will have lost most of its texture and given off all its flavour. Taste the soup and season it. If you have used a knuckle of bacon it will not need any salt. Thin the soup to the consistency you want by adding stock or water, or water and wine mixed. Or if you want a thicker soup, put it in the food processor or blender, and sieve or not as you wish. For an even more substantial soup, add a few chunks of salami or grilled black pudding or boiling sausage. Bring back to the boil and simmer for a while longer.

This makes a large quantity of soup so I often serve it thick and chunky the first day, then on the second day add a little more stock, sieve it and serve it smooth.

4 thick cod steaks	Black pepper	*Grilled cod*
1 tablespoon olive oil	Salt	*with water-*
1 tablespoon lemon juice	Watercress purée (see p. 134)	*cress purée*
		SERVES 4

Dry the cod steaks. Mix the oil, lemon juice, salt and pepper and brush all over the cod. Grill under a very hot grill for 2–3 minutes on each side, depending on thickness.

Heat the watercress purée and serve the cod steaks on a bed of purée with a few steamed potatoes, new ones if you can get them.

Follow with a salad of shredded Chinese leaves, raisins and walnuts, dressed with oil and lemon juice.

Grapes and
grapefruit
SERVES 4

Grapes from the southern hemisphere are available in winter. Remove the seeds from a small bunch and cut them in half. Slice two grapefruits and cut off the rind and pith. Lay two or three slices of grapefruit on each plate, pile some grapes on top, sprinkle with the juice from the end slices of grapefruit. Chill and serve completely natural, no sugar or liqueurs if you can.

MONKFISH IN PASTRY
GLAZED ROAST DUCK
WHITE CHOCOLATE MOUSSE

Looking back, I see that for some considerable while my roast duck was quite a favourite for dinner parties or Sunday lunches. Then I seemed to get out of the habit of cooking roasts and it doesn't appear in my diary after the beginning of 1980. A pity, for duck is tasty and this method avoids the problem of the excess fattiness.

A Mâcon-Prissé would go well with the monkfish, and with the duck I might serve a claret from a smaller property, a *cru bourgeois* such as Château Cissac or Château les Ormes-de-Pez. There is no wine which goes well with chocolate.

Monkfish in
pastry
SERVES 4 AS A
STARTER, 2 AS A
MAIN COURSE

Monkfish prepared this way looks like beef Wellington and is quite a surprise for your guests when you slice into it. An individual fillet makes an interesting and tasty first course.

1 lb / 450 g thick fillet of
  monkfish
½ lb / 225 g button mushrooms
1 onion
1 oz / 25 g butter

2 tablespoons chopped parsley
2 oz / 50 g smoked ham,
  chopped
12 oz / 350 g puff pastry

Trim all the skin and membrane from the monkfish. Slice into four neat fillets. Wipe dry. Make a *duxelles* by finely chopping the onion and frying in the butter. Then add the finely chopped mushrooms. I find the food processor ideal for this purpose. Cook the vegetables together until soft and resembling a purée. Cool. Heat a non-stick frying pan and fry the fish fillets for 30 seconds on each side. Cool. Pat dry with paper towels.

Roll the pastry out and cut into four pieces of the size and shape to completely enclose the fish plus filling. Spoon an eighth of the mushroom mixture on to the pastry. Flatten and place a fillet on top. Spoon an eighth more of the mixture on top, flatten and sprinkle with the ham and parsley. Fold the pastry over and seal. Brush with milk or beaten egg. Prick the top with a fork. Prepare the other fillets in the same way. Place on a damp baking sheet and bake in a hot oven gas mark 6, 200°C/400°F, for 15–20 minutes. Serve on heated serving plates with a wedge of lemon and a bunch of watercress. Hand a little melted butter, hollandaise sauce or white butter sauce separately if you wish.

On reflection, I think I probably devised this dish to use up a large bottle of Southern Comfort we'd bought for some reason or another. Similarly sticky liqueurs would probably be adequate substitutes.

Glazed roast duck
SERVES 3 OR 4

1 fresh duck weighing about
    5–6 lb/2½ kg
3 cloves garlic
1 orange
Salt, pepper, paprika
1 tablespoon clear honey
3 tablespoons Southern
    Comfort

For the stuffing
8 oz/225 g cooked rice
Some or all of the following,
    chopped or sliced:
Celery
Spring onions
Apricots
Prunes
Walnuts
Apple
Ginger
Herbs and seasoning

Remove any loose fat from the cavity or neck end of the bird. With a skewer or sharp-pointed knife, prick the skin all over, particularly in the fatty parts. This is most important as it allows the fat to drain off during cooking, leaving a crispy glazed skin. Cut the garlic into slivers and insert into some of the slits in the skin. Sometimes I would insert slivers of ginger too, instead of putting it in the stuffing. Cut the orange in half. Rub the cut orange all over the skin to dampen it, then sprinkle salt, pepper and paprika all over the duck. Let it sit for an hour or two to absorb the flavours. (I have left it in the fridge overnight.) Squeeze the orange and blend the juice with the honey and liqueur. Heat the oven to gas mark 7, 220°C/425°F. Stuff the duck and secure the cavities closed with toothpicks or put in a couple of well placed stitches with kitchen thread. Brush well with the orange juice mixture.

Take a clean roasting pan and rinse it. Place a wire rack on top and then put the duck on it, on its side. Cook at gas mark 7, 220°C/425°F, for 10 minutes. Turn the oven down to gas mark 5–6, 190–200°C/375–400°F, for 20 minutes. Remove the duck from the oven. Turn the heat back up to gas mark 7, 220°C/425°F. Brush the duck all over with the orange juice. Turn the duck over. If a lot of fat has been given off, you should drain it into a container. Return the duck to the oven and cook for 10 minutes at gas mark 7, 220°C/425°F, then 20 minutes at the lower temperature. Remove from the oven. Raise the temperature once more to gas mark 7, 220°C/425°F. Turn the duck on to its back, draining off any more fat. Brush all over with plenty of orange juice. Replace in the oven and roast for 10 minutes at gas mark 7, 220°C/425°F, then 20 minutes at gas mark 5–6, 190–200°C/375–400°F. Baste once more during the cooking time. Remove from the oven and let it relax for a few minutes. Carve and serve with some of the stuffing, plus a green salad.

If there are more cooking juices than fat in the bottom of the roasting pan, use them to make a gravy, adding any remaining basting mixture. Or use the liver, neck, wing pinions etc. to make a rich stock which could be your gravy base if there are no cooking juices.

A little jelly such as rhubarb or gooseberry would go well with the duck.

White chocolate mousse
SERVES 4–5

This is one of the richest, wickedest puddings I know, and even those who say they are not keen on chocolate don't have to be persuaded to try it. If you can get fine Swiss chocolate, so much the better. In desperation I have used Milky Bars, which also worked.

7 oz/200 g white chocolate   2 tablespoons double cream
3½ oz/100 g dark chocolate   3 size-3 eggs, separated
2 oz/60 g butter

Melt the white chocolate in the cream, either in a basin over hot water or in a heavy based pan. Remove from heat. Add the butter and beat it in quickly. Stir in the lightly beaten egg yolks. Whisk the egg whites and fold into the chocolate. Pour into individual pots and chill.

Once the mousse has begun to set, pour on just enough melted dark chocolate to cover the surface and let it go hard. Garnish with a crystallised violet or some finely chopped orange peel. In fact, the dish stands well on its own without any decoration. The top will be hard, a shell which must be broken to get to the creamy mousse underneath.

WINTER SALAD
CASSEROLE OF TRIPE
HARICOT BEANS
ENGLISH APPLES AND CHEDDAR CHEESE

Tripe is one of the most underrated, undervalued, tasty, nourishing dishes known to man. My favourite way of doing it is to cook it very slowly, with tomatoes, onions, belly pork and a pig's trotter. The end result is a wonderfully satisfying, rich tasting but, in fact, very digestible stew which I serve with haricot beans cooked with herbs and white wine. This is a dish fit to serve to anyone, but do make sure first that your guests like tripe. Sadly, few people do.

With this drink Taunton cider or a simple *vin du pays*. Cook the tripe and beans in it too.

Who wants to pay £1 for an imported Iceberg lettuce in the winter? *Winter salad* Usually that is all we can get in the way of traditional salad herbs; the soft, hot-house variety are hardly worth the bother of taking out of their polythene bags. So with a dearth of salad things we need to look at other greens. Chinese leaves are worth bothering with. They are quite expensive, but there is little waste and they keep well in the salad drawer of the refrigerator. Spinach, cabbage, endive, celery tops and chicory are all good additions to the salad bowl. To precede a dish of tripe I would serve a crisp salad to which I'd add some nuts, raisins and cubes of cheese, the whole served with a quite mustardy dressing.

Casserole
of tripe
SERVES 4

Enlist your butcher's help for this dish. Honeycomb tripe looks best, if you can get it. And ask to have the pig's trotters split down the middle.

2½ lb / 1 kg tripe
4 oz / 100 g belly pork
1 or 2 pig's trotters
2 onions
1 tin of tomatoes

4 cloves garlic
Small bunch of fresh herbs
½ pint / 300 ml stock or dry
   cider
Seasoning

Wash the tripe well and scrape off any fat. Cut into 2 in / 5 cm squares and dry very thoroughly. Trim the rind off the belly pork and cut the meat into chunks or strips. Heat it in a casserole and let the fat run. In this quickly fry the tripe, a few pieces at a time, until just beginning to brown. Remove and set aside. Cook the pieces of pig's trotter in the same way. Remove and put with the tripe. Slice the onions and fry these until brown. Pour over them the tinned tomatoes and bring to the boil. Add the herbs and crushed garlic and return the tripe pieces and pig's trotters to the casserole. Add the stock. Bring slowly to the boil, cover and bake in the oven gas mark 3, 170°C / 325°F, for about 3 hours. Longer will not harm it. Before serving you might like to strain off the juices, reduce them somewhat, season to taste, then return to the pot.

Serve from the pot with baked potatoes or haricot beans.

Haricot beans
SERVES 4

12 oz / 350 g haricot beans
½ pint / 300 ml dry cider or
   white wine

Sprig of rosemary
Salt, pepper and garlic
Twist of orange zest

Prepare the beans as for cassoulet. (See p. 71). Lightly butter an earthenware pot and place the soaked beans inside. Bring the cider or wine to the boil with the herbs, seasoning and orange zest and pour over the beans. Cover and cook in a low oven alongside the tripe.

I usually serve fruit and cheese after a casserole.

SOME THOUGHTS ON LEFTOVERS

Omelettes, soufflés, soups and pancakes are good vehicles for using up leftovers. But do use good leftovers – mushrooms, sweetbreads, game, non-soggy vegetables, fruit sauces etc. – and use your imagination.

Let us say, for example, that you have a fairly elaborate dinner party one Saturday night. One course is a homemade ravioli, the main course is, perhaps, a wild duck or some pigeons. Roll out, while still soft and pliable, the extra dough you will certainly have left over from the ravioli. Cut it into quite wide strips. A pastry cutter gives a nice fluted edge but this is not essential. You can quite happily leave this to dry overnight and it will keep a few days if need be. Then use your leftover game for a fine sauce. Chop it up and add to lightly fried mushrooms and finely chopped shallots with a spot of red wine and any leftover gravy, and you have pappardelle with game sauce. Leftover hare turns this into a classic Italian dish.

Leftover fish makes a good cold mousse, and if you have good quality gelatine or aspic, you can make a very attractive dish. You might serve the mousse in individual ramekins, decorated with a sprig of herbs and covered with a thin layer of jelly.

If I have served a whole turbot or sole, and because I haven't cooked it too long, I always feel there is lots of flavour left in the bones and I simmer these, together with a carrot, onion and celery, finely chopped, for 20 minutes or so to make a good fish stock.

If I have any pheasant left over ever, I put it in the food processor with a fair amount of butter, some juniper berries, a sprig of rosemary and a drop of port or vermouth. Processed until smooth, then potted, this is a good starter for another day, served with hot toast and, perhaps, some homemade pickles.

I commented earlier on using good quality leftovers, not limp or soggy things. However, one day, I broke all the rules and still made a very good summer soup. I put in the blender the remains of a mixed salad – tomatoes, cucumber, lettuce, watercress, radicchio, spring onions, stoned olives – with its dressing. By now the lettuce was decidedly limp. To each soupbowl I added a couple of ice-cubes, some fresh basil, and a spoonful of good olive oil to float on the top. It was quite excellent and a dish in its own right, not a collection of leftovers.

One thing we frequently have left over is chicken: not because we don't like it much but because the average chicken is too much for two people. My favourite way of cooking it is to pot roast it (see p. 114), and there will usually be a good bit of breast left. Potted chicken is nice for sandwiches or as a filling for crêpes. To make this, take equal quantities of cooked chicken and butter. Process with salt, pepper, mace and a little lemon juice. Pack into small ramekins. Cover with melted butter, clarified if possible, to seal.

A cold chicken mousse can be made with the addition of a good stock and gelatine, cream and lemon juice (just a touch). Put in the processor for a minute and then fold in a couple of stiffly whipped egg whites to lighten it.

Buttered rice is one of our favourite dishes with a pot roast chicken, so next day you could serve an excellent, rich cream of chicken soup. Remove the leftover meat from the carcass, which you put in a pot with about 2 pints or a litre of water, and whatever you wish to add to flavour the stock – a chopped carrot, onion, celery, leek, parsley stalks, watercress, mushroom stalks. Simmer for an hour or two. Sieve, cool and refrigerate. Next day, skim off all the fat. Bring the stock to boiling point, reduce a little, add single or double cream and some *beurre manié* (½ oz / 15 g) to thicken. Shred or chop the leftover chicken and add it, with a tablespoon of leftover rice, to the stock. Serve very hot. Garnish with a thin slice of lemon.

The remains of a cheeseboard can provide the makings of individual soufflés. Use some of the more unusual cheeses – goat's cheese, Roquefort, Camembert – added to a basic soufflé mix (see p. 21). But singly of course, so that the distinctive flavour is retained.

Cooked broccoli or courgettes made into a purée are also very suitable for soufflés, particularly if you enliven them with a garlic and anchovy sauce which you make by crushing two or three cloves of garlic with four anchovy fillets and heating gently in an ounce of butter and two tablespoons of olive oil.

Turning to puddings made from leftovers, I am more cautious here, or perhaps just lacking in imagination. I am not sure that trifle *is* best made using stale cake. That seems to me a little lacking in respect. I'm not sure that I would use stale cake for anything except bird-food.

On the other hand, I do remember once making a spectacular pear charlotte from leftover caramel pears (p. 69) and extra honey cream (p. 103) by making a purée of the pears, folding in the cream and a ¼ pt/150 ml pear juice (apple would do as well) in which I had dissolved 1½ sheets of gelatine. I lined an oiled soufflé mould with sponge fingers moistened with a little more juice, filled the space with the pear mousse and, when this had set, poured the caramel sauce on top and again let this set.

Fruit sauces for ice creams, pancakes or sweet omelettes can be made from fresh fruit purées or sieved cooked dried fruit. They can be used also for small soufflés, blended into the basic mixture.

These are just a few ideas on how I use my leftovers. As you will find out for yourself, the possibilities are endless.

SPRING

For me this is really two seasons. There is a winter spring and a summer spring. And, in this most changeable period of the changeable English year, you may get winter spring days after you have felt the first breath of the coming summer.

This changeableness is reflected in what food is available, seasonal. Some years asparagus is a spring vegetable, sometimes an early summer one. From my food diaries I see that in some years we have been eating the first salmon trout in February; other years we have had to wait until Easter. And who now can afford to eat that most seasonal of foods, spring lamb, in its proper season?

It is hard now to resist the imported fruits, the first strawberries from southern Spain, the artichokes from Cyprus, the first of the wild salmon. But you will find yourself paying for the privilege of eating *en primeur*, so this is the time perhaps to make a little go a long way: an artichoke risotto instead of artichoke vinaigrette, salmon tartare as a starter rather than a whole poached salmon.

It is, too, a season which encourages us to think of lighter, sharper food as a contrast to the warm soothing casseroles of winter.

More than at any other time, food shopping in spring is a real adventure. You simply do not know what you will find in the market so you have to be prepared to be flexible, cooking what's available rather than having your menu planned in advance. That is how I arrived at most of the spring meals I describe here.

SALMON TARTARE & GINGER MAYONNAISE
POT ROAST PHEASANT
BRAISED CELERY
ORANGE SALAD

Here I combine the last of the game with the first of the salmon in a menu which is the epitome of winter and spring – you're looking forward and then back, seeing a glimpse of two seasons in one meal.

With this meal serve the best white burgundy you can afford.

Salmon tartare
& ginger
mayonnaise
SERVES 4

½ lb / 225 g salmon fillet
1 small onion
Salt
Pepper
2 tablespoons vodka (optional)

For the mayonnaise
1 egg yolk
¼ pint / 150 ml sunflower oil
½ coffeespoon chopped, fresh
   ginger
Juice of ½ lime or lemon
½ teaspoon good mustard
Pinch of sugar, salt or pepper

Place the fish in a non-metal bowl, skinned and roughly chopped, with the sliced onion, seasoning and vodka if you are using it. Let it stand for half an hour or so in the fridge. (The timing on this is not too important and you can happily leave it covered in the fridge all day. The fish will, of course, absorb more of the onion flavour the longer you leave it.)

Prepare the mayonnaise in the way that works best for you; I use a miniature balloon whisk and a teacup. Once the oil and egg has emulsified, add the lime or lemon juice a few drops at a time in between additions of more oil, then add the mustard and finely chopped ginger. Season to taste and set aside, covered until needed. For the final preparation place the fish and onion on a heavy chopping board and chop thoroughly with a heavy knife or cleaver until the fish looks well 'minced'. Season to taste. Do not over-chop or it will turn into a soggy mass. If you use a food processor take care not to over-process for the same reason. The finished dish should have a good texture.

To serve, use pretty, individual, medium-sized plates. Place a couple of spoonfuls of salmon tartare on each plate and a spoonful of mayonnaise. Garnish with a thin slice of lime or lemon, a few grains of red caviar (lumpfish roe), a sprig of watercress, or a few thinly sliced onion rings. A sweet pickle goes well with this, either a slice of pickled cucumber, a gherkin, or a sprig of pickled samphire (see p. 146 for pickle recipes).

Hand pumpernickel or brown bread and butter separately or, even better, serve two or three miniature potato pancakes on the plate.

Potato pancakes

¾ lb / 350 g potatoes	1 egg
1 small onion	½ pint / 300 ml water
2 teaspoons cornflour or arrowroot	Pinch of salt
	½ teaspoon oil

Peel the potatoes. If you are going to use a food processor, roughly chop them and the onion, then put into the bowl with the water and the salt and process until quite fine. Pour into a basin and leave for 15–20 minutes. If you are using a grater, shred the potato as finely as possible into a bowl, add the salt and water and leave for 15–20 minutes. You will find that the potato, and the starch given off, will have sunk to the bottom and the liquid will be quite clear. Pour off the liquid carefully and stop pouring when you reach the cloudy sediment. Beat into this the egg, oil, cornflour and salt. Heat a thick frying pan or griddle, oil lightly and when smoking drop in a soupspoon of the well-stirred potato batter. With a large pan you can probably cope with three or four pancakes at a time. Turn over after about a minute, by which time the base should be cooked and golden. Cook on the other side for a further minute and remove to a plate or wire rack. Test the first one for done-ness, which will depend on how coarse or fine the potato is. Carry on until all the mixture has been used up. Keep them warm by covering with a teatowel and standing the plate or rack over a pan of hot water.

Pot roast pheasant

SERVES 4

A hen pheasant, being smaller than a cock, will serve three people well, whilst a cock will serve four. However, a hen is tastier, so cook two and use the leftovers to make a game sauce to serve with pasta the next day. If you decide to use spirits, Calvados will go well with apples, and whisky adds an unusual and pleasant flavour.

2 plump hen pheasants	½ lemon
½ oz / 15 g butter	2 onions
Spirits – optional	2 good quality apples
Seasoning	

Heat the butter in a heavy casserole. Sear the pheasants all over. Flame, if you are using spirits. Lightly season and squeeze on a few drops of lemon juice. Peel and slice the onion and apple and add to the casserole. Turn the pheasants on to the breast to keep them juicy, cover and cook in a pre-heated oven gas mark 3–4, 175°C/350°F, for 50–60 minutes.

When cooked, remove the onions and apples, drain off the juice and put all in the blender or through a sieve. The mixture should be thick enough to need no *liaison*. Carve or joint the pheasant and serve with a little of the sauce, some redcurrant or cranberry jelly and some celery hearts which you could braise in the oven while the pheasant is cooking. Cook the celery in a buttered dish, lightly seasoned with salt and pepper and sprinkled with 4 tablespoons of water or stock. Cover with a butter paper or foil.

Orange salad   A very simple dish of skinned and thinly sliced oranges is perfect at this time of year because the oranges are at their very best, from Morocco and Spain. A sprinkling of orange flower water will add an unusual touch.

SPAGHETTI WITH MUSSELS
SWEETBREAD TART
SPINACH AND CELERY SALAD
PEAR SORBET WITH POACHED PEARS

A favourite meal which combines many of our favourite foods — pasta, shellfish, offal, greens and fruit.

A crisp, young, white Rioja would be excellent here. We like the Marqués de Murrieta very much.

Spaghetti with mussels
SERVES 4–6
AS A STARTER,
2–3 AS A MAIN
COURSE

This recipe adapts perfectly to other types of pasta and to other types of shellfish. Clams, cockles or queen scallops are all excellent with pasta.

1 lb/450 g pasta – see p. 25	2 cloves garlic
2 lb/900 g mussels	1 oz/25 g butter
Small glass of white wine	2 tablespoons chopped parsley

Scrub, scrape and wash the mussels, discarding any which remain open. Put into a lidded saucepan with the white wine. Cover and steam on a high heat for 2–3 minutes. Remove from the heat. When cool enough to handle, remove the mussels from their shells and set aside. Strain the liquor into a saucepan. Boil it fiercely to reduce it. Crush the garlic and mix it with the butter.

Cook the pasta according to the directions. Drain the pasta and toss in the garlic butter. Add the mussels, the sauce and the chopped parsley. Toss once more and serve immediately.

Sweetbread tart
SERVES 4

8 oz / 225 g shortcrust pastry
2 oz / 50 g streaky green bacon
1 lb / 450 g prepared, blanched sweetbreads, calves' or lambs', see p. 38 for preparation
4 oz / 100 g button mushrooms
5 fl oz / 150 ml double cream
Seasoning
Lemon zest

Roll out the pastry. Line a quiche dish and bake blind. Remove from oven and keep it warm. Meanwhile, cut the bacon into strips and cook in a frying pan. Slice the sweetbreads and add these to the pan, stirring and letting them just begin to take colour. Wipe the button mushrooms and add them to the pan together with the cream. Simmer for 10 minutes or so. Taste and season. Stir in the lemon zest and pour the filling, very hot, into the pastry case. Serve immediately, with a fresh spinach and celery salad, using young, tender spinach leaves and thinly sliced celery with a tangy dressing.

Pear sorbet with poached pears
SERVES 4–6

6 large ripe pears
Juice of a lemon
Eau-de-vie-de-poire – optional

Peel the pears, cut in half and remove the core. Put in a heavy pan with the lemon juice. Poach until soft. Remove from the pan and cool. Make a purée from four of the pears and freeze this mixture, stirring from time to time if necessary. Slice the remaining four halves and arrange on dessert plates. Serve with a scoop of sorbet, sprinkled, if you like, with *eau-de-vie*.

CREAM OF ARTICHOKE SOUP
SCALLOPS WITH GINGER & SPRING ONIONS
STEAMED VEGETABLES
ORANGE SORBET

A warming soup followed by a light dish of scallops and vegetables and a fresh-tasting orange sorbet to finish.

A dry, sparkling Saumur, an inexpensive yet elegant alternative to champagne, would be in keeping with these light textures and flavours.

Cream of artichoke soup
SERVES 4–6

2 lb / 900 g Jerusalem artichokes
2 pints / 1 litre vegetable stock
4 tablespoons double cream
2 tomatoes
1 stick celery, chopped

1 carrot, chopped
1 small onion, chopped
½ oz / 15 g butter
1 tablespoon oil
Salt, pepper, nutmeg

Wash and scrub the artichokes. No need to peel them. Trim off any discoloured or bruised parts. Chop them roughly.

Heat the oil and butter in a large saucepan, gently cook the onion until beginning to colour, add the rest of the vegetables including the artichokes and the stock. Bring to the boil and simmer for 30–40 minutes, until the vegetables are soft. Process, blend or purée, and then sieve into a clean pan, pushing through as much of the mixture as possible.

Bring back to boiling point, add the cream, salt and pepper to taste and a pinch of nutmeg. If the soup is too thick for your taste, thin with a little more vegetable stock, milk or single cream. Serve very hot in heated soup bowls.

Scallops with ginger & spring onions
SERVES 4

12 scallops
Bunch of spring onions
Piece of fresh ginger
Crushed garlic

Soy sauce
Drop of sesame oil – optional, but it does add to the finished dish

The ideal way to cook this is in a steamer on top of another steamer cooking the vegetables, but if you do not have a steamer, use a soup plate which fits over the top of a pan of water.

First wash, dry and clean the scallops, removing the piece of white muscle and the intestine. Wash and trim the spring onions and slice diagonally into 1 in/2.5 cm pieces. Peel the ginger, cut into tiny shreds. Slice each scallop into two or three rounds depending upon thickness. Place the ginger, garlic and spring onions in the bottom of the soup plate and the scallops on top. Sprinkle with soy sauce and sesame oil. Cover with another soup plate and place on top of a pan of boiling water. Steam for a few minutes until the scallops are cooked, but lightly and only just opaque.

Steamed vegetables

These should be prepared just before the scallops as they will take longer to cook.

Some or all of the following:
Fine green beans
Mangetouts
Bean sprouts
Broccoli florets

Mushrooms
Carrot strips
Thinly sliced celery
Shredded Chinese leaves

Pile all the vegetables into a steamer or colander and cook, covered, over boiling water for 8–10 minutes.

Serve a ring of steamed vegetables on each heated plate, and the scallops in the centre.

You could also serve rice with this, brown or white.

Orange sorbet
SERVES 4 OR 5

8–12 oranges – depending upon size and juiciness

2 tablespoons glycerine
1 oz/25 g castor sugar

Stir the sugar into the glycerine and add to the freshly squeezed orange juice. Pour into a plastic box and freeze in the deep freeze or freezer compartment of the fridge. Remove two or three times during freezing, to stir and break down the crystals.

If you have a *sorbetière* or ice cream maker, freeze according to the directions.

SNAIL PUFFS
BEEF IN WHITE WINE
GRATIN OF POTATOES AND MUSHROOMS
GREEN SALAD
CHEESE AND FRUIT

This is a meal which looks after itself and needs no last minute finishing off so would adapt well to feeding larger numbers if you double or triple the quantities. There is little in it which is typical of spring, except that I feel it provides a comforting, warming dinner party for good friends on one of those days when summer still feels far away.

I am not sure of the origins of snail puffs but I first tasted them cooked by my friend Margaret Andrews, an excellent, extravagant cook whose meals and company we enjoy enormously. Tinned snails are the only ones I have ever used for this dish. For guests who do not like snails, I fill the puff pastry cases with button mushrooms or prawns. You could also use some chopped sweetbreads, but in my experience, people who don't like snails often don't like sweetbreads either.

A Provence wine would be good with this meal, a Bandol Domaine des Templiers perhaps.

Snail puffs
MAKES 12

½ lb / 225 g puff pastry 3 oz / 75 g garlic butter
1 doz medium-sized snails

Roll out the pastry and cut into twelve 3 in / 7.5 cm squares. Place a snail in the centre of each, with a portion of the garlic butter. Make this by mashing crushed garlic into salted butter. Season with pepper, a little salt and add finely chopped parsley. Dampen the edges of the pastry, fold the corners to the centre and pinch to seal along the four edges, completely enclosing the snail and its butter. You can prepare to this point well in advance, in the morning or even the night before. Refrigerating the pastries does in fact help them to remain sealed tight during baking.

When ready to bake, brush with beaten egg yolk and place in a pre-heated oven, gas mark 6, 200°C / 400°F, for 12 minutes.

These are good served hot before dinner with aperitifs.

This is based on the traditional casserole dish from the South of France, the white wine giving it an unusually light flavour, the olives and lemon adding piquancy.

Beef in white wine
SERVES 4–5

Marinade
½ pint / 300 ml dry white wine
1 tablespoon olive oil
1 stalk of celery
1 carrot
1 onion
Parsley stalks
Zest of half a lemon
2 cloves of garlic – crushed
Pepper

1½ lb / 700 g lean braising steak
2 oz / 50 g piece of belly pork
1 onion
6 oz / 175 g black olives
3 peeled, deseeded and
    chopped tomatoes
Chopped chives

Chop the celery, carrot and onion and add to the other marinade ingredients in a deep bowl. Trim the meat, cut it into 1 in / 2.5 cm chunks and mix well into the marinade. Leave for several hours, but preferably overnight.

Remove the meat from the marinade which should then be strained and the liquid saved. Dry the meat thoroughly on paper towels. Cut the belly pork into strips. Gently heat a heavy casserole, add the belly pork and render it slowly until it gives off fat. Raise the heat and cook the sliced onion until golden brown. Remove the onion and pork and keep to one side. Keeping the fat at almost smoking point, sear the pieces of beef all over, a few at a time. Do not crowd in the casserole as this lowers the heat and the meat, instead of searing, will begin to steam. When all the meat has been seared, return it to the casserole with the onions and pork. Add the olives, pour on the strained marinade and bring slowly to the boil. Cover and cook in a medium oven gas mark 4, 180°C / 350°F, for 2 hours, when the meat should be tender. Just before you are ready to serve, stir in the tomatoes and chives and taste for any extra seasoning.

2 oz / 50 g butter
1½ lb / 700 g potatoes, peeled
    and sliced no more than ¼
    inch / 5 mm thick

1 lb / 450 g mushrooms, wiped
    and sliced
Salt and pepper
¼ pint / 150 ml stock, cream or
    milk

Gratin of potatoes and mushrooms
SERVES 4–5

Thickly butter a gratin dish and cover with a layer of sliced potatoes. Next add a layer of mushrooms. Dot with a little more butter. Continue with another layer of potatoes and so on. Season. Pour the liquid over and cover with foil or a butter paper except for the last twenty minutes.

Bake for 1½ hours below the beef casserole.

A crisp salad, followed by cheese and fresh fruit or fruit salad is all you need to end this satisfying meal.

FRESH PASTA WITH FENNEL & SCALLOPS
MACKEREL WITH MUSTARD & CORIANDER
WATERCRESS SALAD
ZABAGLIONE

I like the structure of an Italian meal which offers you complementary rather than contrasting dishes in sequence, where it is quite in order to serve a fish dish followed by another fish dish. Such a meal, particularly when it contains pasta, our other favourite food, suits us perfectly.

Marino Superiore or Frascati are two Italian wines which would accompany these dishes well.

Fresh pasta with fennel & scallops

SERVES 4 AS A STARTER, 2 AS A MAIN COURSE

See p. 25 for the ingredients and method of making fresh pasta.

See p. 25 for the ingredients and method of making fresh pasta.

Filling

6 scallops – choose those with the largest brightest corals you can find
½ oz / 15 g butter
2 small shallots
½ stick celery
Small fennel bulb

¼ pint / 150 ml strong fish stock
2 heaped tablespoons *fromage blanc, quark, crème fraîche* or double cream
Seasoning to taste

Stamp out circles of pasta dough.

Wash and dry the scallops thoroughly. Remove the coral and set aside. Cut the scallops into tiny cubes. Lightly fry the finely chopped shallots, fennel and celery in the butter. Cool. Mix with the scallops.

Season lightly. Place a spoonful of filling in the centre of each circle. Moisten the edges and fold over to seal in a half circle. Allow to dry. Cook in the usual way. Meanwhile make the sauce by blending the uncooked roe with the stock and *fromage blanc* or cream. Heat gently to prevent it from curdling. Spoon some on to each plate and lay five or six drained pasta shapes on top.

Mackerel are at their very best in winter and spring. This dish can be cooked in the oven or under the grill.

Mackerel with mustard & coriander
SERVES 4

4 mackerel fillets
2 tablespoons french mustard
Juice of half a lemon
4 tablespoons finely chopped
  coriander

1 tablespoon olive oil or
  softened butter
Salt and pepper

Wipe the fillets. Mix the rest of the ingredients together and spread over the mackerel fillets. Bake in a hot oven for 12 minutes or grill. A few fresh breadcrumbs or some oatmeal could be sprinkled on top just before cooking to give a crunchy effect.

Serve a watercress, chicory and orange salad to follow.

I hesitate to suggest this as the pudding. It requires eggs, and eggs are also used in the pasta. However the quantities work out at about half an egg each in the pasta and a little more for the pudding, so I think no great harm will be done and the Italian flavour of the meal is maintained with this traditional dish. I have to admit I cannot remember ever having had it in Italy. If you do not have marsala in your store cupboard, port, madeira or sherry would be adequate substitutes, but you may need to add a little more sugar.

Zabaglione
SERVES 4 OR 5

4 tablespoons marsala
1 oz/25 g castor sugar

3 egg yolks
2 egg whites

Put the wine in a pudding basin over a pan of hot water, which should be maintained just below boiling point. Add the sugar and let this melt. Then add the eggs and extra egg yolk. Begin whisking and keep whisking until the mixture is frothy and much increased in volume. Serve hot, in long-stemmed wine glasses, with sponge fingers.

LEEKS VINAIGRETTE
RACK OF LAMB WITH THREE MUSTARDS
JERUSALEM ARTICHOKES AU GRATIN
RHUBARB FOOL

At this time of year you can find thin, young leeks which make an excellent hors d'oeuvres. I once bought a two kilo bundle in the market in Marseilles early one January. The leeks were almost pencil thin and, cooked this way, were every bit as good as asparagus. My father presents this dish in a slightly different way, with slices of fried black pudding. It sounds an odd combination, but it works.

Claret is a traditional accompaniment to lamb and although our lamb is unlikely to have grown up in the salt meadows of Pauillac, north of Bordeaux, it is the wine from this commune that we most like to serve with roast lamb.

I see from my food diary that in 1974, when I served this lamb dish to celebrate our wedding anniversary in December, it was accompanied by a 1964 Château Latour. It was indeed shameful to drink it so young, but fortunately we let it breathe for some hours and thoroughly enjoyed it. At £5.99 a bottle we were drinking history. We had the good sense to keep a few bottles, but it will be a rare occasion indeed that will deserve one.

Château Lynch-Bages produces wines which we enjoy very much – big, flavourful, robust in the 1976 vintage.

The Pauillac co-operative produces La Rose Pauillac which is extremely good value, having all the characteristics of the wine of Pauillac, and is probably the best buy for regular drinking. However, all wines from the Pauillac and neighbouring communes of Saint-Julien and Saint-Estèphe, as well as elsewhere in the Médoc, are now really out of reach for everyday drinking for all except the lucky few. Because of this we often turn our attention to the Cabernet Sauvignon wines of other countries. In some cases those too are far beyond the average pocket. I'm thinking here of the fine 1974 vintage in California which produced remarkable wines. We are the lucky owners of a few bottles of Robert Mondavi Cabernet Sauvignon but again, it will take a grand occasion to induce us to open one.

4–6 thin leeks per person
  (fewer if you can only find
  the stouter ones)
Olive oil

Freshly ground black pepper
Sea salt – if possible
A squeeze of lemon

Leeks vinaigrette

Trim and clean the leeks carefully. Split lengthways down towards the base but without cutting right through. Rinse and drain. Drop into boiling, lightly salted water and cook until quite tender, 5–10 minutes depending on size. Alternatively, you can steam them. Drain and arrange in a shallow dish. While still warm, sprinkle fairly liberally with good olive oil, a small squeeze of lemon juice, salt and pepper.

I would serve them while still slightly warm. Preparing them in advance and refrigerating them never seems quite as successful. The leeks begin to look dull and their flavour is not improved.

This is a simple, quickly prepared dish that is a good standby. On the other hand it is good enough to serve as a starter to quite a grand main course, particularly a rich one. It is also a dish which can be dressed up, if not with slices of black pudding, then perhaps with cubes of good salami.

The three mustards are not essential, but it gives it a nice ring in French – *carré d'agneau aux trois moutardes*, and the blend of mustards does provide an interesting, subtle flavour. I use plain Dijon mustard, tarragon mustard and mild sweet mustard. Two best ends of lamb will give 2–3 cutlets each for 4 people. Use as much garlic as you like, and if you are unable to get fresh herbs, dried herbs will give sufficient flavour.

Rack of lamb with three mustards
SERVES 4

2 best ends or loin of lamb
4 cloves of garlic
2 tablespoons of mustard

Salt and pepper to taste
Pinch of fresh thyme,
  marjoram or rosemary

If you buy best end, have the butcher chine it, the chine being the split backbone, which you then remove before carving either into slices or chops. Remove the thin skin and most of the fat from the joint.

Crush the garlic with the salt and pepper and mix with the mustard and herbs. You could add a little oil and lemon juice to produce a spreading consistency. Spread the mixture between the cutlets and over the flat surface. Place on a rack in a roasting tin and roast in a hot oven for 20–25 minutes. The outside should be quite dark and crisp, the inside, pink and juicy. Naturally you will cook it for longer if you prefer your lamb well done. Remove from the oven and let it rest in a warm place for five minutes.

With this serve Jerusalem artichokes, baked for about the same amount of time but on a lower shelf in the oven.

Jerusalem artichokes au gratin
SERVES 4–6

2 lb / 1 kg Jerusalem artichokes   1 oz / 25 g butter
7 fl oz / 200 ml thin cream or   Salt and pepper
   thin béchamel sauce

This may seem a large quantity for four, but because of all the knobbly bits, there is often quite a lot of waste with Jerusalem artichokes. I find that if you scrub and wash them well, cutting off any bruised knobs, it is not necessary to peel them. Since making that discovery, I have served Jerusalem artichokes quite often. Their sweet nutty flavour, combined with their substantial but non-starchy texture makes them a very good accompanying vegetable for those who want a change from potatoes.

Cut the vegetables into ¼ in / 5 mm slices and drop them into a large pan of boiling water. Bring back to boiling point and then simmer for 2–3 minutes. Drain. Butter an ovenproof dish and put in a single layer of artichoke slices. Season lightly and pour on a few tablespoons of cream or *béchamel*. Continue with the next layer of artichokes and carry on until you have used them all up. Finish with more cream or sauce on top. Bake on a low shelf in the oven for 25–30 minutes.

Rhubarb fool
SERVES 4–6

1½–2 lb / 700–900 g rhubarb   ½ pint / 300 ml double cream
   stalks   1 egg white
Sugar or honey to taste

Traditional recipes suggest that a fool should have a custard base, so if you make good custard, you could substitute it for the cream and egg white I use.

Trim the rhubarb at the root end and remove any leaves. If the fruit is young and tender, as it should be, you will not need to 'skin' it. Cut into 1 in / 2.5 cm chunks. Steam or simmer until soft. Drain and cool. If using a blender or processor, process until smooth. Otherwise mash it up with two forks until it is a soft mass. Sweeten, but not too much. The rhubarb should retain a pleasing tartness.

Whisk the egg white until stiff. Whisk the cream likewise. Fold the cream into the fruit purée and then fold in the egg white. It is important that the purée is cool if you are using cream, otherwise it will melt. Spoon into glass dishes or pretty wine glasses and chill.

SMOKED FISH PÂTÉS AND CRUDITÉS
SEAFOOD LASAGNE
WINTER SALAD
ORANGES IN SYRUP

With this very Italian flavoured meal I would want to serve some lively Italian wines. And the liveliest of all for a starter is a Prosecco – from Valdobbiadene or Conegliano, to the north of Venice. It is white, sparkling and with a flavour all of its own and can be dry or medium. The latter is good on its own, as an aperitif perhaps, but the dry is best with a meal. To follow, a young Marino; Gotto d'Oro is crisp and dry, a good partner for the seafood lasagne.

For this a food processor is invaluable.

Smoked fish pâtés and crudités
SERVES 4–6

1 smoked trout
4 oz / 125 g smoked salmon
  pieces
1 smoked mackerel fillet
3–4 oz / 100 g polyunsaturated
  margarine

1 carton thick, natural yoghurt
Zest of a lemon
Pepper
Chopped parsley or chives

Start with the most delicately flavoured fish first and you will not need to wash out the food processor bowl between each operation. Put the flesh of the trout into the processor with one-third of the margarine and yoghurt. Grate on a little lemon zest, add seasoning and chopped herbs. Process until smooth and pack into a white china ramekin. Do exactly the same with the salmon and the mackerel. Chill. Serve the three pâtés together with brown bread and a bowlful of fresh crudités – radishes, cauliflower florets, spring onions, strips of celeriac, carrot and celery sticks, blanched green beans – whatever you can find.

Seafood lasagne
SERVES 4–5

Because the fish filling for this dish cooks rather more quickly than a meat filling would, you need to pre-cook the lasagne for slightly longer than you would normally.

This is a dish which can adapt itself to suit your pocket and your fishmonger. I have served it as the main course at a dinner party using scallops, mussels, prawns and monkfish. Cod or haddock would work well because they are fairly firm-fleshed fish; whiting fillets would simply break up and go soft. Turbot or sole would be a great treat no doubt, but I would hesitate to use such fine, delicately flavoured fish in this way. I have yet to try something like smoked haddock but I feel it would work well. I imagine that oilier fishes such as mackerel and herring would not be successful. Whatever fish I choose, I always add some shellfish – prawns, mussels, scallops – for the extra flavour and different texture.

½ lb / 225 g lasagne sheets –   2 oz / 50 g butter
   dried, fresh or homemade   1 tablespoon oil
1½ pints / 900 ml thick   2–2½ lbs / 1 kg fish
   béchamel sauce   Seasoning

Butter very liberally a rectangular oven-to-table dish. I use an old, rough, glazed, deep earthenware dish bought ages ago which does the job perfectly.

Bring a large pan of water to the boil, add 1 teaspoon of salt and a tablespoon of oil to stop the pasta sticking. Drop in the lasagne sheets two or three at a time (not more, as they may stick together). Cook for 8 minutes if fresh, 6 minutes if homemade, and according to the directions on the packet if dried, plus 2 minutes. Drain and set aside. Cut the fish, as appropriate, into chunks of about 1 in / 2.5 cm. Dry very thoroughly, as most fish gives off quite a lot of liquid as it cooks.

Make a thick béchamel sauce using fish stock, single cream or milk. Spread a few spoonfuls on the bottom of the dish and place on it a layer of lasagne. Then put a layer of fish on the lasagne, cover this with more sauce and another layer of lasagne. Continue until you have used up all the fish and all the lasagne. (You may like to keep the different fish in separate layers, or mix it all together.) The top layer should be the last of the béchamel. Place towards the top of a medium hot oven and cook for 30 minutes until brown and bubbling on top. Serve at once.

Vegetables are not served with fish dishes in Italy. I think a crunchy winter salad would be just the thing after this – plenty of Chinese leaves and cabbage, plus a few raisins and carrot strips.

7 oranges – at least two of which should have good, unblemished skins	¼ pint / 150 ml water 4 oz / 100 g sugar	*Oranges in syrup* SERVES 4–5

Make up a syrup with the sugar and water. First let the sugar melt in the water over a low heat, then cook more fiercely until syrupy but not coloured.

While the syrup is cooking, peel and thinly slice five of the oranges, using the end slices for juice. Remove some of the peel of the two remaining oranges (with a grater or a zester). This dish looks particularly nice garnished with long strips of peel and to obtain this you really do need a zester, dangerous implement. The first time I used one to make this dish I finished up with grazed knuckles and marmalade. Squeeze the juice from these two oranges. Add the juice to the syrup and cook until syrupy once more. Add the zest and cook for no more than a minute – any longer and it begins to taste like marmalade. Cool.

Arrange the orange slices on a pretty plate or glass dish and pour the syrup over them.

NETTLE SOUP
ROASTED CALVES' LIVER
SPINACH AND DANDELION SALAD
HOT LEMON SOUFFLÉ

Here is a meal full of sharp, tangy flavours to enliven the tastebuds, and plenty of iron and vitamins to enliven the blood. The green things are served either raw or very lightly cooked to retain their goodness, and fresh lemon zest is grated on to the soufflé at the last minute.

I first had calves' liver cooked this way by Karin Perry, a friend, neighbour and truly excellent cook. It took me some time before I found the courage to have a go myself – a large piece of calves' liver represents a considerable financial investment and one needs to be sure of what one is doing.

German wines have the crispness, fruitiness and acidity to stand up to all the flavours of this meal. They remain very good value and I would probably serve a 1976 Rheingau of which there seems still to be a quantity about. We have some from 1983 to look forward to when all the 1976 is finished.

Nettle soup
SERVES 4–6

This is very much a spring recipe to be cooked when nettles are still young. Wear gloves and pick only the topmost tender leaves and shoots.

1½ pints / 900 ml good rich stock – chicken or vegetable
2 oz / 50 g pearl barley

Sprig of fresh thyme or rosemary
2 oz / 50 g fresh nettles

Bring the stock to the boil, throw in the barley and the herbs. Reduce the heat and simmer until the barley is tender. Remove the herbs. Season to taste. Add the nettle shoots, return to the boil; remove from the heat and serve immediately.

You might like to serve this soup with tiny dumplings instead of pearl barley.

Roasted calves' liver
SERVES 4–6

2 lb / 900 g calves' liver, in one piece
Seasoning

Small wineglass of port or madeira or dry vermouth – optional

Wash and dry the liver, snipping out any pieces of piping. Butter a loaf tin, terrine or earthenware dish. Place the liver in it, folding and shaping to fit, so that the top is a smooth surface. Season lightly, pour on the wine if using it, cover with a buttered paper and bake in a pre-heated oven gas mark 5, 190°C / 375°F, for 25–35 minutes, depending on how pink you like the liver. Carefully lift on to a serving plate and allow to rest for 5 minutes or so. Slice on the plate and serve with the cooking juices.

A purée of parsnip and garlic would be delicious with this. I also serve a small glass dish of jelly – cranberry, bramble, quince – see p. 145.

Once again you want the youngest, tenderest dandelion leaves and very fresh spinach.

Spinach and dandelion salad
SERVES 4

2 oz / 50 g smoked streaky
  bacon
Spinach

Fresh dandelion leaves
½ lemon

Cut the bacon into matchsticks. Render it slowly in a frying pan, then cook more quickly to allow it to crisp.

Quickly wash the greens and shake or towel them dry. Tear the spinach into manageable pieces. Place it with the dandelion leaves in a salad bowl. Pour on the hot bacon and its fat, and toss quickly. Squeeze on a little lemon juice and serve immediately.

1½ oz / 40 g butter
1 oz / 25 g flour
1 oz / 25 g castor sugar
¼ pint / 150 ml milk

2 lemons
3 eggs
1 oz / 25 g bread or cake
  crumbs

Hot lemon soufflé
SERVES 4

Melt 1 oz / 25 g butter and stir in the flour and sugar. Mix to a thick sauce with the milk. Cook for 7–10 minutes on a gentle heat. Cool. Beat in the juice of one and a half lemons and the grated zest of one. Separate the eggs. Beat in the egg yolks. Whisk the egg whites and fold into the lemon sauce. Butter a soufflé dish or four individual ones and sprinkle with the crumbs. Fill to within ¼ in / 5 mm of the top with the soufflé mixture and put the dish or ramekins into a *bain marie* (or a roasting tin containing ½ in / 1 cm of water) and place in the middle of a medium hot oven for about 25 minutes (15, if using small ramekins).

Just before serving, grate some lemon zest on the top.

CARROT AND MINT SOUP
ROAST LOIN OF PORK WITH APRICOTS
PEAR TARTS WITH MARZIPAN

To me this is a Sunday lunch type of meal, with the closest thing I do to a traditional Sunday roast.

How about a Californian wine? A Cabernet Sauvignon or a Zinfandel from one of the small wineries such as Robert Mondavi?

Carrot and
mint soup
SERVES 4–5

1 lb / 450 g carrots	Few sprigs of mint
1 onion	¼ pint / 150 ml single cream,
1 stick of celery	buttermilk, smatana or
½ oz / 15 g butter	yoghurt – optional
1¼ pints / 700 ml stock	Seasoning

Peel and slice the vegetables. Heat the butter in a heavy pan and cook the vegetables lightly. Add the stock and most of the mint. Simmer until the vegetables are tender. Press through a sieve or blend in the food processor. Season to taste. Add the cream etc. if liked and serve very hot garnished with a few mint leaves.

Roast loin of
pork with
apricots
SERVES 4

3½ lb / 1.5 kg loin of pork	3 oz / 75 g dried apricots,
1 onion, chopped	chopped
4 oz / 100 g breadcrumbs	2 oz / 50 g walnuts, almonds
Fresh herbs – whatever you	or pinenuts
have available	Seasoning
	Stock to moisten

First skin the joint and then bone it or have your butcher do it for you. You should have a large piece of skin, a sizeable rectangular cushion of meat with a loose flap, and an assortment of bones. Make stock with the bones. Trim off the loose flap of meat. Mince this or finely chop it and mix with the onion, breadcrumbs, herbs, apricots, nuts and seasoning. Make two horizontal parallel cuts in the meat, without cutting right through. Stuff each opening and shape into a roll. Tie at intervals to keep it together.

Seal all over in a non-stick frying pan and transfer to a casserole. Moisten with a few spoonfuls of stock, cover with the piece of skin and cook in a slowish oven gas mark 3–4, 170–180°C / 325–350°F for 1–1½ hours. Remove from the oven and carve into slices. Serve with the cooking juices.

Braised leeks are a good vegetable with this dish.

Pear tarts
with marzipan
SERVES 4

12 oz / 350 g pastry	4 pears
4 oz / 125 g marzipan	Glaze – apricot jam or
(see p. 19)	redcurrant jelly

Roll out the pastry and line four individual tartlet tins, about 4–5 in /

10–12 cm in diameter. Prick the base. Soften the marzipan and spread this over the tart base. Peel the pears and slice lengthways. Arrange in a flower petal shape around the pastry. Brush the glaze over the fruit and bake towards the top of the oven at gas mark 4, 180°C/350°F, for 12–15 minutes.

RAVIOLI AL MAGRO
FISH FILLETS IN SPINACH
GREEN SALAD
PEARS IN HONEY

Another unusual stuffed pasta dish, tasted this time in Milan, appropriately enough in Lent, for the filling is not made from meat, fish or fowl, as its name indicates. Once more, no recipe could I find, but almonds and ricotta were certainly in it. The green colour was harder to identify, brighter and paler than spinach. I have found that blanched outer lettuce leaves achieve the desired effect, but cannot be sure how authentic this is.

Since this is a Lenten meal, let's drink sparkling mineral water!

Pasta	*Filling*	*Ravioli al magro*
5 oz / 150 g plain flour	6 large lettuce leaves	SERVES 4
2 oz / 50 g fine semolina	2 oz / 50 g ricotta or cottage	AS A STARTER,
2 size-3 eggs	cheese	2 AS A MAIN
	2 oz / 50 g ground almonds	COURSE

Make up the pasta dough as described on p. 25. Remove any tough, thick centre spine from the lettuce leaves. Wash and drain in a colander. Pour boiling water over the leaves to blanch them. Dry them thoroughly. Either by hand or in a food processor, blend the three ingredients together, chopping the lettuce leaves finely first.

Stamp out circles of pasta, place a spoonful of filling in the middle. Dampen the edges, fold over, pinch and seal. Drop into boiling salted water and boil quickly until done but still *al dente*.

These can be served plain and perhaps should be, since this is a Lenten dish. Otherwise a little melted butter, or single cream and freshly grated Parmesan would be in order.

Fish fillets
in spinach
SERVES 4

You may be lucky enough to get some of the first of the salmon trout, but this recipe works equally well with fillets of baby halibut, sole, plaice or lemon sole.

4 skinned fillets weighing
    5–6 oz / 150–175 g each
8 large spinach leaves, or
    Swiss chard with the central
    stem removed
Seasoning

4 ripe tomatoes
¼ pint / 150 ml good strong fish
    stock
½ lb / 225 g leeks
Cream and butter to finish the
    sauce – optional

Wash and blanch the leaves, then dry them. Wipe the fish fillets and season lightly. Skin, deseed and chop the tomatoes. Divide into four and spoon one portion on to the middle of each fillet, skinned side uppermost. Fold the ends of the fillet over the tomato to enclose it. There will be a tendency for the tomato to seep out at the sides, but push as much back in as possible. Once the fillets are wrapped all will be enclosed in a neat parcel.

Spread out the spinach leaves, taking two for each fillet. Overlap any splits and place the folded fish on top of the leaves. Fold the spinach around the fish into a parcel with no tears in it. Place in a buttered or non-stick dish that will go on top of the stove as well as in the oven. Continue until you have four parcels. Pour the stock over the fish. On top of the stove bring it just to the point where the stock begins to bubble. Transfer immediately to a pre-heated oven gas mark 4, 180°C / 350°F, and cook for 8 minutes.

Meanwhile wash the leeks carefully and shred into matchstick-sized pieces. Blanch or steam them quickly until just tender but not soggy.

Remove the fish from the oven when it is cooked. Drain the liquid into another pan and keep the fish warm. The fish and tomatoes will have given off cooking juices and so diluted the stock. Reduce this over a high heat until it thickens. At this point you can enrich with cream and butter if you wish. Place a fish parcel on each plate, surrounded by a little sauce and garnished with shredded leeks.

A salad of curly endive or Chinese leaves dressed with olive oil and orange juice would follow this.

I often cook pears in red or white wine but in keeping with the Lenten purity of the menu, perhaps we should banish the alcohol.

4 pears
Juice of a lemon

4 dessertspoons clear honey

Peel the pears but leave the stalks on. Rub them all over with the cut lemon. Squeeze the juice into a pan and add the honey. Heat and melt the honey then put the pears into the pan. Cover and cook on a low heat until tender. Serve warm with the juices poured over.

POTATO AND CABBAGE SOUP
STUFFED SQUID
GREEN SALAD
PINEAPPLE WITH LIQUEUR

This meal reminds me of the dinners we have eaten in the Bairro Alta or in the Alfama, the old quarters of Lisbon. One of our favourite cities, we usually seem to visit it in the spring, so I feel able to include the menu in this section of my book. However, I am sure it would be equally appropriate in the autumn or winter. It is not a *grand luxe* meal, but simple and tasty. We have a dear friend who eats in the finest restaurants in the world and to whom I like to serve my best, but somewhere in the meal, however grand, I have to find room for a dish of stuffed squid which he claims is one of his favourites.

Squid is perhaps not the first thing you might choose from the fishmonger's slab, but I find it is well worth the trouble to prepare it. Once cleaned and skinned it can be cooked in a variety of ways, the most common being to chop it up and serve it in a paella or risotto, in a stew using its own ink to thicken and flavour the sauce, or sliced into rings, battered and deep-fried. Cooked properly, it is tender, sweet and full of flavour. Overcooked, it is tough and not worth bothering with. For this recipe I use the small ones, sometimes called arrow fish. The larger ones I find better for stewing or deep frying.

Vinho Verde, the crisp, dry, slightly *pétillant* Portuguese wine would be quite in keeping with this meal and almost certainly what we would drink in Lisbon.

Potato and
cabbage soup
SERVES 4–5

The fresh coriander leaves give an authentic Portuguese flavour to this soup. If they are not available, use parsley or watercress. The stock can be vegetable or chicken but particularly good for potato soup is one made from a not-too-salty knuckle of bacon.

1 rasher of smoked bacon or	6 oz / 175 g cabbage
1 dessertspoon olive oil	Fresh coriander leaves
1 small onion	1½ pints / 900 ml good stock
½ lb / 225 g potatoes	

Cut the bacon into matchsticks and render it in a heavy pan. Or heat up the oil. Slice the onion and fry in the fat until lightly coloured. Meanwhile peel and dice the potatoes. Turn these in the pan and cook without burning them. Shred the cabbage and add to the pan. Pour in the stock, bring to the boil and simmer until the vegetables are tender.

There are two ways of proceeding from here. One is to serve the soup clear, with a few leaves of coriander floating in it. The second is to take out three ladlefuls of the vegetables, mash them and return to the soup to thicken it, at the same time adding the coriander. Either way is good.

Stuffed squid
SERVES 4–5

16–20 squid about 5–6 in /	⅛ pint / 75 ml white wine
12–14 cm long	8 oz / 225 g cooked rice
2 tablespoons olive oil	Seasoning
1 onion	Fresh coriander leaves or
3 cloves garlic, crushed	parsley
2 tomatoes – fresh or tinned	

First of all clean the squid in the sink. Tip them all into a colander and rinse them. One at a time, holding the body of the squid in one hand, pull the head off (the tentacle end) with the other. Cut the tentacles off and set aside. Now deal with the body. Peel off the mottled skin and remove the two triangular flaps. Put these with the tentacles. Feel inside the cavity and remove the 'backbone' which looks like a strip of soft clear perspex. Then squeeze the cavity like a tube of toothpaste to remove anything left inside. Rinse and set aside. Continue with the next and so on until you have a little pile of white pockets waiting to be stuffed. It takes longer to write about than actually to clean one. Chop the tentacles and the flaps.

Heat a tablespoon of olive oil in a frying pan. Peel and finely chop the onion. Cook in the oil for a few minutes then add the chopped tentacles, flaps and garlic. Stir until the squid becomes opaque. At this point add the chopped tomatoes, the seasoning, some of the herbs and the cooked rice. Mix in and remove from the heat. Allow to cool. Spoon the rice mixture into the squid, until loosely stuffed. Secure the end closed with a cocktail stick or toothpick.

Butter or oil a flat ovenproof dish and lay the stuffed squid in a single layer. Pour the wine over and trickle the rest of the olive oil on top. Cover with foil or a butter paper and bake in the middle of a pre-heated oven gas mark 4, 180°C/350°F, for 10 minutes.

Serve, sprinkled with more fresh herbs, straight from the baking dish, with a green salad to accompany it.

Pineapple with liqueur

At this time of year most of our fruit is imported so none of it will be very fresh. To choose a pineapple, first of all make sure the outer skin is not blemished and bruised. Then smell it. If it smells pineappley, it's ripe.

Peel and slice. (Two slices per serving is generous.) Remove the core if this seems tough. Sprinkle on a few spoonfuls of liqueur or spirits left over from Christmas. *Eaux-de-vie* such as maraschino or framboise are good; slivovic too or grappa; some of the sweet orange liqueurs or Drambuie. I'm not sure that Tia Maria would be right however.

PASTA PRIMAVERA
BRAISED PORK WITH ONIONS
ORANGE AND MANGO IN GINGER WINE

You will find the ingredients for this meal towards the end of the spring when the first of the spring vegetables are in the shops. We first tasted *pasta primavera* not in Italy but in a restaurant run by a Genoese ex-ship's steward in New York's Upper East Side. We started off with clams, went on to the pasta, followed by a large veal cutlet prepared Milanese style, and were complimented on our Italian appetites afterwards. Truly we might have been in Boccadasse, the fishing village on the outskirts of Genoa.

We drank a full-bodied red Italian wine with this meal, but was it a

Barolo, a Bardolino or a Brunello di Montalcino? Any one of these would suit.

Pasta primavera
SERVES 4–5
AS A STARTER,
2–3 AS A MAIN
COURSE

The essence of this dish lies in the freshness of the spring vegetables and the quality of the pasta. You can use tagliatelle, but I find fusilli (the spirals) go particularly well with chunks and slices of vegetables. I suggest some vegetables below but you may prefer others – broccoli florets and sliced celery instead of carrots and mushrooms, for example.

1 lb / 450 g pasta
2 or 3 new carrots
3 oz / 75 g mangetouts
Bunch of spring onions
3 oz / 75 g thin green beans
4 oz / 100 g button mushrooms
or oyster mushrooms
(*pleurottes*) if available

2 tablespoons olive oil
4 tablespoons stock
2 tablespoons *pesto*
or
2 tablespoons finely chopped
chives or parsley and 2
cloves garlic, crushed
Fresh Parmesan

Prepare all the vegetables. Slice some, cut others into chunks. Heat the olive oil and turn all the vegetables in it; cook gently for four or five minutes until lightly cooked but not coloured. If you are using mushrooms and spring onions these should be added near the end of the cooking time. Mix the stock with the *pesto* or herbs and garlic. Add to the vegetables and cook uncovered for a minute or two longer so that a good sauce is formed.

Meanwhile, cook the pasta according to whether it is homemade, bought fresh or dried. Drain. Toss with a little more olive oil, salt and black pepper and tip into a large serving dish. Season the vegetables to taste and pour them over the pasta. Toss again and serve immediately, separately handing round freshly grated Parmesan.

*Braised pork
with onions*
SERVES 4

This dish calls for spare rib chops (not to be confused with spare ribs) which are chunky and tasty chops. But be sure to ask for lean ones.

2 lb / 900 g spare rib chops
12 oz / 350 g smallish onions
2 or 3 cardamom pods –
optional but they give a
pleasing flavour

2 oranges
Seasoning
Parsley or chives

Remove any rind and excess fat from the chops. Heat a heavy casserole and render a small piece of fat, enough to lightly oil the surface. Peel the onions and cook in the casserole. Remove and set aside. Raise the heat, sear the chops on both sides and remove. Open the cardamom pods and drop the seeds into the casserole. Cook them for a minute or two and return the onions and the meat to the pot. Grate the zest from the two oranges and keep half for garnish. Squeeze the oranges into the casserole adding some of the zest. Cover and cook in a medium oven gas mark 4, 180°C / 350°F, or on top of the stove for 45–60 minutes or until the meat and onions are tender. Garnish with chopped parsley or chives and the orange zest and serve with or before a crisp salad.

I see nothing wrong in carrying through the orange flavour to the end of the meal if you like oranges.

Orange and mango in ginger wine
SERVES 4

4 oranges
1 ripe mango

4 tablespoons ginger wine
Flaked almonds – optional

Slice the oranges and cut off the pith and skin. Peel and slice the mango. Arrange prettily on individual serving dishes. Glass dessert plates show up fruit very well. Mix the juice of the end slices of orange with the ginger wine and spoon over the fruit. Scatter with flaked almonds, which are even better if you toast them first.

POTS, PANS, PLATES AND PARSLEY

I would like to be able to describe the ideal *batterie de cuisine*, but I'm not sure what that is. I only know what works for me and what doesn't, what I would like to have in my kitchen, and what I can do without.

Although I grumble sometimes that our kitchen is too small, its size does impose a useful discipline in that it scarcely contains anything which is not used. Four frying pans, when I claim to fry very little? Well yes, because with the exception of my latest non-stick frying pan which is fast becoming one of my most used utensils, the others are cast iron in different sizes, well seasoned and thus practically non-stick themselves and used for crêpes, omelettes, fish, reducing sauces etc.

Enamel pans I find no good for me because I tend to cook over a very high heat. However my large frying pan with the cracked enamel now has a new life as a steamer. I half fill it with water, place an open steamer basket in it, and steam my fish on it, covered with the domed lid of yet another frying pan long since vanished from my kitchen. Because our water is very hard I keep another old, worn-out enamel pan solely for boiling eggs in. Do this in a good pan and you soon ruin it with the layer of calcium that forms. My soup pan is a heavy aluminium one given to me by my mother. I can remember her ordering it from a catalogue over 30 years ago. It is indestructible and never burns or sticks.

Knives I acquire all over the place, although the ones I use most are a small, sharp, steel knife for vegetables and the fiddlier boning tasks, and a large, old, bone-handled cook's knife that's well over a hundred years old and belonged to my great-grandmother.

You see, I have a penchant for secondhand items. I like to think that someone else has enjoyed using them over the years. My collection of china plates reflects this too. These are all shapes and sizes, all beautifully painted and designed. In some the gilt and flowers are fading but I still use them to serve a gâteau, to hand round dried fruit and sweets at the end of a meal, or stuffed vine leaves at the start. My coffee cups are of the same sort of antiquity.

When it comes to the plates on which I serve my starters and main courses, there I am something of a purist. So that it will not clash with the colours of the food, I use plain, creamy white, hexagonal plates. Food that has been prepared with care and attention deserves a passing glance at least. It pleases the olfactory sense; it will please the palate; why should it not also be pleasing to the eye? Many people seem to think that serving a fillet of turbot or a breast of duck on *top* of its accompanying sauce is one of the more pretentious aspects of *nouvelle cuisine*. I could not disagree more. Covering with a sauce shows neither off to best advantage.

It is all too easy to garnish a dish that doesn't require any decoration. I find I have to guard against this tendency sometimes. Not that I'm tempted to make roses out of tomato skins and waterlilies out of radishes, but there is an occasional, injudicious use of chopped parsley or chives. Then again, some garnishes add an integral flavouring – nutmeg sprinkled on some pasta dishes, parsley, lemon and garlic on *osso bucco*, coriander in certain soups. These are important.

Gadgets in the kitchen? Things I wouldn't be without? My small, heavy, steel pasta machine which rolls out thin sheets of pasta for raviolis and tortellinis and cuts tagliatelle, tagliarini and spaghetti. A simple piece of well-made machinery, easy to clean and a joy to use.

My blender is much used for soups and fruit purées; an older generation electric coffee grinder is now used for nuts and spices. I'm beginning to think that I ought to consider one of the second generation food processors. The one I have now does very good work mincing meat, chopping vegetables, mixing pasta dough, slicing carrots, grating hard cheese and making bread dough and pastry, but I rather fancy something bigger and with different speeds.

After much hesitation I finally bought an inexpensive *sorbetière* in the summer and I'm very glad I did. Ice creams and, particularly, sorbets have rightfully come back into favour. A few years ago I would not have felt I was really trying hard if I served sorbet to my guests at the end of a meal, but fortunately I have realised how versatile and delicious they are, and how welcome and acceptable instead of a richer pudding. So a *sorbetière* isn't a piece of luxury equipment I can do without.

A freezer? A microwave? Not for me.

SUMMER

Lighter food is the order of the day; not necessarily cold food, which can get very boring for the cook and guest alike if served day in, day out. But you will find here lots of fish recipes, and where there are meat recipes they will often be for small portions. Pasta dishes too appear with their seasonal sauces, for pasta is a year-round dish. Here, it comes in satisfying, yet delicate guises. And because there are cold miserable days in the summer, some versatile soups are included which will use up any excess of vegetables. Thicker versions make sauces.

If the weather is hot, however, fast methods of cooking are the most useful. You won't want long, slow stews, or roasts that require the oven to be on all day. So, many of my suggestions for summer are cooked on the hob or grilled. Quick frying, poaching and steaming are the methods best suited to all the fresh produce available which, if it is not to be eaten raw, should be cooked as quickly as possible.

Puddings are almost exclusively based on fruit. Fruit purées are useful as sauces for bought-in ices, as a base for sorbets, or to be poured over yoghurt, ricotta or *fromage frais*.

A well-stocked herb garden comes into its own at this time of the year – french tarragon, sweet basil, chervil, coriander and sorrel are the most rewarding to grow, as they accompany so well many of the traditional summer foods such as salmon, tomatoes and soups.

FRESH ASPARAGUS WITH EGGS
GRILLED DOVER SOLE
SALAD
STRAWBERRY HEARTS

I see that one year we ate asparagus every day for a week, went to Spain for two weeks, then ate it almost every day for the next four weeks. The English asparagus season is not that long, so I must assume that we started off by eating imported asparagus before we went on to the local stuff. Because the season is so short, and because we like it so much, it is no hardship to eat it day after day.

Usually I serve it warm with melted butter, cold with mayonnaise or sauce mousseline or, to provide a slightly more substantial dish, I serve bundles of freshly cooked asparagus on warmed plates on to which I have first slid a poached or a lightly fried egg. The sauce is the egg yolk into which you dip the asparagus points. Simple and delicious. A plain grilled fish follows this perfectly.

A white English wine would be most appropriate; Elmham Park, Adgestone and Biddenden are all wines we've enjoyed recently.

Grilled Dover sole
SERVES 4

4 small Dover sole, skinned
2 oz / 50 g butter

1 tablespoon finely chopped fresh herbs

Heat the grill. Blend the butter with the herbs. Make a slit down the backbone of the fish. Ease the flesh away on both sides of the bone and spread in a little of the herb butter. Close the flaps. Repeat on the other side. Place foil under the rack in the grill pan to collect any juices. Grill the sole for 2–3 minutes on each side. Serve with cooking juices poured over, plenty of fresh parsley and steamed new potatoes.

Strawberry hearts
SERVES 4

At the height of the asparagus season, strawberries are still very expensive. This recipe makes a few go a long way.

1 small punnet of strawberries
4 heaped tablespoons of one
   or a combination of
   cottage cheese, *fromage
   blanc, fromage frais, crème
   fraîche*, cream cheese

4 teaspoons castor sugar
2 egg whites

Wash the strawberries quickly. Reserve four for garnish. Blend the rest with your chosen cream mixture and sugar. Whisk the egg whites and fold into the purée. Line heart-shaped, pierced moulds with damp muslin and spoon the mixture in. Place the moulds on a tray or dish to catch the excess liquid which drips through, and refrigerate for at least one hour, more if you wish. To serve, unmould each one on to a pretty dessert plate. Remove the muslin very carefully, garnish with strawberry halves and a mint leaf. If you have plenty of strawberries, you could purée a second punnet with a little liqueur and surround the heart with this sauce.

CHILLED SALMON AND CUCUMBER SOUP
POT ROAST CHICKEN
GREEN SALAD
COMPÔTE OF PLUMS

As well as a balance of colour and texture in a meal, a balance of temperatures is important too. You don't often want all hot or all cold dishes, even in the summer. This meal presents a nice compromise – a chilled soup, a hot main course and a warm or tepid pudding. On a really miserable, cold, wet summer day, I might be tempted to heat the soup. And if it was one of those rare scorching hot days, I would cook the chicken and the plums in the morning before it got too hot to do the cooking, and then let them cool quickly. The compôte I would then served chilled, the chicken cold. But a normal English summer day will accommodate the dishes as I have suggested them – chilled, hot and warm.

A dry, white Graves would go well with the soup and the chicken – inexpensive, widely available and usually reliable. Château Olivier would be nice for a special meal.

Chilled salmon and cucumber soup

SERVES 4

If you give your fishmonger enough notice he will be pleased to save bones for you to make stock. You can also use cooked bones from the salmon trout terrine (p. 121).

1 pint / 600 ml of fish stock
½ peeled small cucumber, the freshest you can find
2 shallots or spring onions

9 oz / 250 g cooked salmon or salmon trout
2–3 tablespoons good yoghurt or *fromage blanc*
Seasoning to taste

Method I: If you like a very smooth, creamy soup, simply put all the ingredients in the blender in two batches and process until smooth. Sieve or not, according to your taste.

Method II: If you like a little more texture to your soup, grate or chop the cucumber, reserve a few flakes of fish and process the rest of the ingredients. Sieve and add the chopped cucumber and pieces of fish.

Fish stock

2 pints / 1½ l water
2½ lb / 1 kg fish bones and
  pieces
Handful of parsley stalks
1 chopped carrot
1 chopped onion
1 chopped celery stalk

1 tablespoon chopped fennel –
  optional
White pepper
1 small piece each of orange
  and lemon zest
1 teaspoon oil

Heat the oil in a large heavy pan – it should just cover the surface, to stop the vegetables and fish sticking to the pan. When hot add the chopped vegetables and stir to stop them burning. When they are just beginning to colour, add the chopped-up fish bones and pieces. Remember, if you have fish pieces amongst the bones, to remove any chunks of fish. These can be added to the soup later. When the fish bones begin to turn opaque, add the water, the pepper, the peel and the parsley stalks. Bring slowly to the boil. Simmer for 40–60 minutes. Strain. Boil, reducing by one third and strain again. Chill.

*Pot roast
chicken*

SERVES 4–5

Pot roasting keeps poultry and game birds moist, succulent and tasty and I now use this method not only for chicken but for guinea fowl, pheasant, partridge and even small turkeys. You can then vary the flavourings, using, say, gin to flame the turkey and adding a few juniper berries, or brandy for the partridge and stuffing with a few muscat grapes.

The problem arises when you start to hunt for good chicken. Much has been written about what it takes to get a chicken ready for the supermarket deepfreeze, what they're fed on, what they're injected with. I avoid them. I find the flesh soggy, dense and lacking any good chickeny flavour. Look for free range farm chickens. If they've been fed on good things, they'll taste good. Like us, they are what they eat. I am lucky enough to be able to buy maize-fed chickens. Most of these are imported from France but I notice one or two more local suppliers. Let us encourage them.

Try to use new season's garlic for this dish.

1 2½–3 lb / 1–1½ kg chicken
1 whole head of garlic
1 oz / 25 g butter, margarine or
    1 tablespoon oil
1 sliced onion

½ lemon
Salt, pepper
2 tablespoons brandy –
    optional
Sprigs of fresh tarragon

Prepare the chicken the day before, or a few hours before cooking. Untruss it. Cut off the wing pinions, remove any loose skin and any fat from the cavity and the neck end. Wipe all over. Peel two or three of the garlic cloves and cut into thin slivers. Insert these at intervals, with a knife point, under the chicken skin. Rub all over with the cut lemon, sprinkle with salt and pepper and place the lemon in the cavity. Put it in the fridge and allow the lemon and garlic to permeate the chicken.

Heat the oil or butter in a large iron or enamel casserole. Add the sliced onion and fry gently. Put the chicken in the pot, breast side down. Allow to colour and then turn it on to the other breast. When this is sealed, turn it over on to its back. Pour on the brandy, if you are using it, and flame. This adds flavour, burns up some of the fat, and the alcohol is consumed by the flames, so it does you no harm. I always use a drop of spirit if I have to cook an ordinary, battery-raised chicken. A good corn-fed chicken needs very little adornment however. Add as much tarragon as you like or can afford (our local delicatessen sells it for £1 or more, a fairly small bunch at that) and the rest of the peeled garlic cloves. Reserve a small sprig of tarragon to finish off the dish. Place the covered casserole in a pre-heated oven gas mark 4, 180°C / 350°F, and cook for 15–20 minutes. Check it for doneness by poking a sharp knife point into the thickest part of the thigh. The juices should run clear.

You will find that the chicken will have made its own juices and the garlic and onion will be soft. From these two ingredients you make your sauce, simply pushing all through a sieve. You can stretch this a little further with some single cream or some chicken stock. Carve the chicken, or cut into four joints, serve with a little of the sauce and some snipped-up tarragon.

Rice goes well with this dish and cooking it in the oven means that it is quite economical. For this, fry a chopped onion or shallot in some olive oil in a casserole, add 6 oz / 175 g Patna rice, stir until covered in oil and add twice the volume of water. Bring to the boil, add a pinch of salt. Put the lid on and place in the oven for 30 minutes. The liquid will be absorbed, the rice fluffy and tender. Serve with the chicken and a green salad.

Make a good chicken stock from the bones and carcass.

Compôte of plums
SERVES 4–5

This dish can also be cooked in the oven, but I suggest you put it in well before the chicken, because it should have time to cool off before you serve it. I always cook more than I need for one meal, serving the rest with cereal at breakfast next day. Use the honey only if the plums are not as sweet as you would like them.

1½–2 lb / 600–900 g ripe plums
Cinnamon sticks or powder
Honey

Wash the plums. Cut round the 'long' circumference and twist each half in opposite directions to separate it from the stone. Place the plum halves in an ovenproof dish. Sprinkle on two or three tablespoons of water, honey to sweeten if you must, and the cinnamon. Cover with foil and bake in a medium oven until tender. Serve if you like with some toasted flaked almonds, or some yoghurt, or both. Or cream. Or ice cream.

ANCHOVY AND CHICORY SALAD
VEAL KIDNEYS IN ROQUEFORT SAUCE
GREEN BEANS
GOOSEBERRY FOOL

This is a quick and easy meal to get together and one that allows you to do some advance preparation. Make the gooseberry fool the day before, or in the morning, using the basic fool recipe on p. 94. Clean and marinate the kidneys overnight. Like all offal, kidneys are best cooked quickly to keep them tender.

Green beans are at their best in the summer. Get the tenderest you can find, and if you grow them yourself, avoid the temptation of letting them grow as big as possible; pick them young and crunchy, not big and fibrous.

Sancerre, Pouilly Fumé and Sauvignon-de-St-Bris remind me of gooseberries. All are firm, assertive wines which would stand up to the rich meat sauce.

Anchovies can be bought in jars or vacuum packed from Italian delicatessens or well-stocked supermarkets. Kept in the fridge once opened, they make a good standby.

Anchovy and chicory salad
SERVES 4

Marinated anchovies
2 firm heads of chicory
1 small, thinly sliced onion
Black olives
Olive oil

Fresh lemon juice
Lemon zest
Crushed garlic
Salt and pepper

Drain 6–8 anchovy fillets per person. Wash the chicory and separate the leaves. On individual plates arrange the chicory like flower petals radiating from the centre. Blend the last five ingredients in the proportions you prefer, into a lemony-garlicky dressing. Place an anchovy fillet on each leaf and the onion rings and olives in the centre. Pour the dressing over the top and serve immediately.

The first time I tasted this dish was at a restaurant in the Avenue Jean Jaurès in Paris, in the heart of the meat market district. Then it was made with the freshest, most delicate lamb's kidneys I have ever tasted. I have never been able to find such good lamb's kidneys here, so make the dish with veal kidneys.

Veal kidneys in Roquefort sauce
SERVES 4

1½ lb / 700 g veal kidneys
1 onion, sliced
2 cloves garlic, crushed
1 tablespoon mild mustard

¼ pint / 150 ml white wine or
  dry cider
2 tablespoons good stock
4 oz / 100 g Roquefort

Remove the skin from the kidneys. Slice into ½ in / 1 cm pieces and with kitchen scissors snip out the fat and gristle from the centre. Marinate for at least a few hours in the wine mixed thoroughly with the mustard, onion and garlic.

When ready to cook, heat a non-stick frying pan. Drain and dry the kidneys, reserving the marinade. Sear the pieces on both sides and cook for 3–4 minutes; the kidneys should still be slightly pink. Remove from the pan and keep warm. Add the marinade to the pan and reduce slightly. Add the stock and reduce a little more. Crumble up the Roquefort and let this melt in the sauce. Return the kidneys to the sauce and heat through. Serve in a flattish, white china dish garnished with chopped chives.

The beans to accompany the kidneys should be steamed or boiled and served while still crisp and bright green. Some broad pasta ribbons would help soak up some of the juices.

It is very easy to overcook offal, so that it becomes tough, dry and unpleasant. I had a disaster with this particular dish when I was planning to serve it to two discriminating guests. The kidneys were cooked just a few seconds too long and I decided they were over-cooked and could not be served in this way. I dashed out to the supermarket but didn't like the look of the lamb chops or the steak on sale. Tom had the brilliant idea of rolling out some fresh pasta dough, chopping the kidney in the food processor, to which I added cream and herbs, and I ended up serving ravioli stuffed with kidneys, accompanied by a Roquefort sauce. It worked.

CHEESE PROFITEROLES AND SALAD
SCALLOPS WITH SAFFRON SAUCE
LAVENDER SORBET

This is a menu for early summer as you must be sure to pick your lavender at its peak, when the buds are full and fragrant and not yet in bloom. No pudding wine will stand up to such a flavour, so with it I serve nothing more than sparkling mineral or spring water. With the rest of the meal I serve a young white burgundy. The Wine Society's St Véran has pleased, as has a Bourgogne Aligoté and a Reuilly. Recently we have enjoyed those of the 1982 vintage; generally speaking, it's the younger the better with less important white burgundies.

Cheese profiteroles and salad
SERVES 4–6

A little strange perhaps having the cheese and salad at the beginning of the meal, but it works. It is fairly substantial, but then we have a light main course. I make the profiteroles in ordinary tart tins, but you could make them smaller, just a teaspoon of the mixture dropped on a baking tray and serve them as pre-dinner snacks. A good vehicle for using up leftover cheese, not just the usual ones, but goat's cheese,

Brie (without the rind) and blue cheese. It is rather wasteful of energy to put the oven on just for a tray of profiteroles, so try and do something else as well – a few bread rolls or a loaf perhaps.

¼ pint / 150 ml milk and water
  mixed
2 oz / 50 g butter
2½ oz / 60 g plain flour
Pinch of salt

2 eggs
2 oz / 50 g cheese – cut up into
  small chunks

Put the butter and liquid into a pan. Gently heat them until the butter has melted. Bring to a strong boil, remove from the heat and tip in the flour and salt in one go. Beat vigorously until the mixture becomes a stiff paste and leaves the side of the pan. Allow to cool slightly. Stir the eggs in one at a time, and keep stirring until the mixture is smooth again. Stir in the chunks of cheese. Butter a 12-tart tin and place a dessertspoon of the mixture in each case. Place in the top half of a pre-heated oven gas mark 6, 220°C / 400°F, and bake for 18 minutes. Switch off the heat, open the door slightly and leave in the oven for a further 3–5 minutes. Serve while hot with small plates of dressed green salad. Before serving, you could, if you wished, slit the profiteroles and slip in a teaspoon of herb cream cheese mixture, or some softened goat's cheese or Roquefort mixed with butter.

This is a very versatile recipe. You can fill the profiteroles with all manner of savouries, or sweet things and serve them as a pudding.

Scallops with saffron sauce
SERVES 4

This dish you will need to cook in the middle of the meal. However, it takes literally 3 or 4 minutes at the most, so you will not find it too inconvenient.

8–12 scallops – depending on
  size
½ pint / 300 ml fish stock
  (see p. 114)
Pinch of saffron threads

½ oz / 15 g butter (or use a
  non-stick frying pan)
2 carrots
Fresh coriander, basil or
  chervil for garnish

Prepare the scallops by separating the coral (also called the tongue or the roe) from the white part. Remove the thin, dark intestine which circles the scallop and the small piece of muscle which toughens during cooking if not removed. Wash quickly to remove any sand and dry thoroughly. Slice each scallop into two rounds. Steep the saffron threads in three tablespoons of the fish stock. Peel the carrots and cut into *julienne* strips. Put them in a metal sieve, colander or basket over a pan of water, ready to steam them lightly at the last minute.

Heat the frying pan, and butter if necessary. When really hot, add the scallops and sear them quickly on both sides. Lower the heat, add the coral and cook for no more than a minute. Remove the scallops and coral and keep them warm. Turn the heat up and add the rest of the fish stock. Reduce by half. Add the saffron liquid. Season to taste. Meanwhile steam the carrots. You may find that the scallops have given off a little more liquid, which you should add to the sauce in the frying pan. You should resist the temptation to enrich the sauce with cream or butter. The scallops have such a delicate texture and flavour that this light saffron sauce will be quite sufficient.

Serve the scallop slices (4 or 6) on a pool of saffron sauce, with the coral to one side, and a little pile of carrot strips to the other. Garnish with one or two leaves of fresh herbs. Spoons should be provided to scoop up the sauce afterwards.

Lavender
sorbet
SERVES 4-6

1 pint/600 ml sugar syrup
Juice of a lemon

2 teacups of washed lavender buds

Bring half the syrup to the boil with the lemon juice. Add 1½ teacups of lavender. Return to the boil then remove from the heat. Let the flowers steep overnight. Next day, strain the liquid into the blender. Add the rest of the syrup and the rest of the washed lavender buds. Process for 30 seconds and strain. Taste. If too sweet, add a little more lemon juice. Freeze or make up in a *sorbetière*.

Serve a small scoop each, garnished with a spray of fresh lavender.

This dish originated on a hot summer's day in my parents' garden in Derbyshire. I had never read about it or tasted it, let alone made it before, but it seemed like a good idea at the time. As, indeed, it was. A perfect ending to a summer meal, it tastes just like it smells.

TERRINE OF SALMON TROUT WITH HERBS
NOISETTES OF LAMB WITH SORREL SAUCE
MELON AND MINT SORBET

A meal full of summer tastes and colours, suitable for a dinner party or a family Sunday lunch. You can prepare the terrine the day before so the final touches for the meal need not take too long. The lamb is, of course, cooked at the last minute.

Looking through my food diaries I see that whenever I have served lamb, whatever the season, we have generally served a good claret with it. Gone are the days of the '67s – Mouton-Rothschild, Pavie and Cantemerle. For a dinner party now we look for the best we can afford.

Terrine of salmon trout with herbs
SERVES 6–8

A dish to be prepared when you've had a surfeit of poached salmon trout at the beginning of the season. It will also work well with salmon and pink trout. I have not tried it with white fish, but sole, turbot or brill lend themselves well to a terrine. Perhaps with brill or pink trout you might need to sharpen up the mixture just a touch with lime or lemon juice. For the herbs I sometimes use a combination, sometimes a single herb. Let us assume we are using three herbs.

2 lb / 900 g salmon trout
½ pint / 300 ml fish stock
  (see p. 114)
½ pint / 300 ml double cream

4 sheets of leaf gelatine
2 tablespoons fresh herbs
2 egg whites

Poach the fish, or wrap in oiled foil and bake in a hot oven for 20 minutes. Allow to cool. Soften the gelatine in the stock according to the directions on the packet.

Blanch the herbs, keeping them separate, by pouring boiling water over them in a sieve. Finely chop and add each herb to one quarter of the cream, to which you will then add three tablespoons of the fish stock with gelatine. Set aside.

Flake the fish and put into a blender or processor with the remaining quarter of the cream and the stock. Process until smooth and sieve. Whisk the egg whites and fold in gently. Season to taste.

Oil a 2 lb / 1 kg terrine and spoon in the first herb mixture, spreading over the base. Allow to set, speeding up this process by refrigerating for a few minutes. Then spoon in half the fish mixture. When firming up, add the second herb cream, and continue in the same way until you finish up with the final herb cream on top. Chill. When ready to serve, unmould the terrine on to a serving plate and serve a slice c each individual plate. This is quite a soft mixture so it is difficult to slice thinner than about one inch. You may or may not want to serve it with a few leaves of salad – watercress and curly endive, a small quantity perhaps.

Noisettes of lamb with sorrel sauce
SERVES 4

If you do not grow sorrel, or have sorrel-growing friends, you may find jars of pasteurised sorrel in good delicatessens. An alternative would be watercress, or perhaps even basil. By June, good strong plants are being imported from Italy, or there are homegrown ones available. Even a parsley sauce would work, but I would add some lemon to this.

8 noisettes of lamb cut from
  the loin
2 cloves crushed garlic
4 fl oz / 120 ml dry white
  vermouth
1 small carrot, 1 stick celery,
  1 small onion – all thinly
  sliced

2½ oz / 60 g butter
¼ pint / 150 ml stock
2 tablespoons cream –
  optional
A handful of shredded sorrel –
  or other herbs as suggested

The night before, trim the lamb of its fat and place in a shallow bowl with the marinade ingredients – the garlic, vermouth, carrot, celery and onion. The dish itself is prepared at the last minute so have all your ingredients to hand so that you don't have to leave your guests for too long.

Drain and dry the pieces of meat, reserving the marinade. Heat up a heavy-based frying pan and add 2 oz / 50 g of the butter. When smoking, put in the lamb, in one layer. Reduce the heat after 30 seconds or so. Cook for 2–3 minutes, raise the heat and turn the meat over. Cook for a further 2–3 minutes, the time depending on how well done you like your lamb. Remove it and keep warm. Deglaze the pan with the marinade and then add the stock. When reduced by half, add the cream, if you are using it, and reduce again. Just before serving add the shredded sorrel and swirl it around in the sauce, which you then finish by thickening it with the remaining $\frac{1}{2}$ oz / 10 g of butter, added a little at a time.

Serve on individual plates garnished with a few lightly cooked vegetables – tiny french beans or broad beans, glazed, baby carrots, courgettes. At this time of the year you have the best available, but do avoid the temptation to overgarnish.

One of the summeriest dishes imaginable! If you can't wait to freeze it, add one measure of vodka or white rum per person, shake over ice, strain and drink through a straw for a delicious summer cocktail.

Melon and mint sorbet
SERVES 4–6

The type of melon you choose will depend very much on availability and at what point in the season you are making the sorbet. Early on the first Galia melons are in the shops, whilst later in the season the honeydew melons are ripe. These two give the lovely green colour. Charentais or cantaloup are delicious too and will give a peachy-coloured sorbet. Whichever you choose, do make sure it is ripe. To test this, all you need do is smell it. If it smells melony, it is ripe. Don't invoke your greengrocer's wrath by squeezing and prodding it. If the melon is very ripe and juicy you can substitute 2 dessertspoons of castor sugar for the syrup. The mint must be fresh; otherwise leave it out altogether.

1 very ripe melon
1 handful fresh mint leaves
4 dessertspoons sugar syrup

Blanch the mint leaves by placing them in a colander or sieve and pouring boiling water over them.

Put all the ingredients in the blender and blend until smooth. Pour into a suitable container and freeze. During the freezing process, you will need to stir several times to stop the mixture crystallising. This recipe works beautifully for those lucky enough to have a *sorbetière* or ice-cream maker.

COURGETTE AND BASIL TARTS
BAKED COD WITH FRESH TOMATO SAUCE
SAMPHIRE
CHEESE AND FRUIT

This is a menu for that time of year when you have a glut of vegetables in the garden; all your tomatoes are ripening off at once and your courgettes seem to be growing before your eyes. For the best flavour, pick them when no bigger than a man's little finger.

Samphire has a short season, July and part of August. If you live near salt marshes you can pick it for free, otherwise your fishmonger may be able to get it for you.

An Alsace Riesling from a reputable shipper would be delicious right through this meal.

Courgette and basil tarts
SERVES 4

These look good as individual tarts served, one to each plate, with a little salad. Alternatively bake one larger one in a quiche dish.

8 oz / 225 g short pastry	¼ pint / 150 ml single cream or
6–8 tiny courgettes	milk
A few sprigs of fresh basil	Salt and pepper to taste
2 size-3 eggs	1 oz / 25 g Gruyère – optional

Roll out the pastry and line four individual tart tins. Prick the bases, line with greaseproof paper, fill with baking beans and bake blind for 5 minutes in a pre-heated oven gas mark 5–6, 190–200°C / 375–400°F. Remove. Meanwhile slice the courgettes paper-thin. Sprinkle with salt and allow to disgorge for a few minutes. Rinse and pat dry. When the pastry is cool, divide the courgettes among the tart cases; shred the basil and sprinkle on top, but reserve a few leaves for garnish. Beat the eggs into the milk or cream. Add the salt and pepper, grated cheese if you wish, then pour the mixture over the courgettes. Bake in the oven for a further 8–10 minutes until done. Serve warm with some shredded basil on top.

Baked cod with fresh tomato sauce
SERVES 4

When I cook cod this way I like to buy the thickest piece from the shoulder. This way I do not run the risk of having it cook dry. Monkfish fillet, haddock and halibut are all good cooked in this fashion.

To make the tomato sauce follow exactly the tomato soup recipe on p. 131 but omit the stock.

2 lb / 900 g piece of cod fillet	Green olives
2 tablespoons olive oil	½ orange
Garlic – 2–3 cloves, to taste	½ pint / 300 ml tomato sauce
Pepper	

Remove the skin and any bones from the fish. Oil an ovenproof dish. Place the fish in it and brush over the rest of the olive oil. Crush or sliver the garlic and tuck it into the fish. Sprinkle with pepper and dot with the green olives. Because the olives are salty you will not need to add extra salt to the dish. Grate the orange zest over the fish, squeeze over it the orange juice. Cover with an oiled paper or foil and bake in the oven at gas mark 7, 220°C / 425°F, for 30 minutes. You will find that the fish gives off some liquid. Drain this into the tomato sauce. Stir it and pour around the fish, having removed the foil. Return it to the oven for five minutes. Serve piping hot, accompanied by a dish of samphire if you can get it.

Samphire

Wash carefully in several changes of water. Remove the root system and discard any bruised or damaged branches. Place in a large pan, pour on boiling water and boil for five minutes. You can also steam it. Drain, serve and eat in the fingers. Some people leave the root on so that you can hold it by the root and eat the tender branches.

This is such an exquisite treat that I often serve it as a course alone, sometimes with melted butter or olive oil. If I can get only a small quantity, I clean it carefully and place it in a clear roasting bag with a large piece of firm fish, seal it and bake it. The flavour of the samphire penetrates the fish in a delicious exchange.

To follow this I serve a piece of cheese and a plate of simple, fresh fruit – peaches and nectarines perhaps, or a plate of soft fruits.

PASTA WITH WILD MUSHROOMS
SALMON TROUT WITH SUMMER SAUCE
SUMMER PUDDING

This is a meal for serving in the height of summer. After Wimbledon the price of salmon and salmon trout comes down. They are plentiful and a good size. I suggest you buy something larger than you need and keep some leftovers for the salmon trout terrine (p. 121) and use the bones and head for the salmon trout and cucumber soup (p. 113). My serving salmon trout rather than salmon is a personal preference. Salmon will do just as well in these recipes, but I find the salmon trout more delicate in flavour, colour and texture.

At this time of year too you can buy raspberries, loganberries and all the currants without feeling too extravagant. I'm sure everybody, somewhere, has their own recipe for summer pudding and most cooks know it off by heart, but I include it as a reminder. It finishes this meal off very well.

Should you want an extra course for a dinner party, why not serve a watercress soup? For this you can use the purée recipe on p. 134 and thin it down with stock and single cream, perhaps sharpening it with a spot of lemon juice.

Although I am not much of a fan of large summer buffets (or large anything, in the way of entertaining) I have to admit that this meal, with one or two additions, has the makings of a summer buffet. Simply buy a larger fish, increase the quantities for the pasta, use a larger basin for the summer pudding and fill it with more fruit, or make several smaller ones. Serve a whole cheese rather than a cheeseboard selection (which can so quickly look untidy and un-appetising). A creamy, unpasteurised Brie on its straw mat would look tempting. Prepare a bowl of green salad using the crispest lettuce you can find (Webb, Cos or Iceberg) to delay the inevitable wilting process. A dish of new potatoes, cooked and served warm in their skins and tossed in olive oil, some coarse sea salt and snipped chives or dill would be perfect.

This is all plain, tasty, filling food. Good rather than new or exciting. But a buffet is usually an adjunct to an occasion, not an occasion in itself. Things other than the food are more important.

With the meal I would like champagne. All the way through. Supermarket champagne will do if I can't have Krug. But all the way through. And pink.

There are some lucky people who have their own secret patches of *chanterelles* which they go back to year after year, bringing in some of their spoils on a Monday morning perhaps, but answering evasively your questions of 'Where did you go this weekend?' Those not so fortunate can use a few dried mushrooms which, though initially expensive, do go quite a long way after soaking. You can also use cultivated mushrooms or perhaps a mixture of these and dried mushrooms. Occasionally greengrocers import *cèpes*, *chanterelles* and *mousserons* from France, at great expense. However, one supplier based in East Anglia I think, is now importing oyster mushrooms – *pleurottes* – from Holland. These brown or grey mushrooms have a succulent texture and delicate flavour when lightly cooked. I buy them whenever I can, and they are particularly good in this recipe. For the pasta, use chunky shapes that hold a sauce – fusilli (spirals), conchiglie (shells) or penne (quills), for example. It is difficult to say how much olive oil you will need, it depends on how much the pasta absorbs, and you need a tablespoonful for the onions and mushrooms.

Pasta with wild mushrooms
SERVES 4

8 oz / 225 g pasta	Olive oil
2 shallots or small onions, peeled and sliced thinly	Crushed clove of garlic
4 spring onions	Juice of half a lemon
6 oz / 175 g fresh mushrooms	Salt and black pepper

Cook the pasta by the method appropriate to the type of pasta you have. Drain it, rinse quickly in cold water, drain again and toss in 4–5 tablespoons of olive oil. Pour the pasta into a wide shallow dish.

Cook the shallots or onions in a tablespoon of oil. Wipe the mushrooms, slice them and add them and the garlic to the pan. Cook quickly without burning. Toss in the sliced spring onions for a few seconds. Spoon the mushroom and onion mixture into the pasta. Turn it thoroughly, adding more oil and garlic if liked. It should be fairly glistening with oil. Squeeze in the lemon juice, sprinkle on a pinch of salt and some freshly ground black pepper.

This is best served warm or just cold, but not refrigerated. Keeping it in the fridge spoils the texture of the pasta as it tends to go stodgy and rubbery. The chilling also kills the flavour.

Salmon trout
SERVES 4

My preferred way for cooking this is to wrap it in foil and bake it in a pre-heated oven. A fish kettle I find rather less successful, but perhaps I just haven't got the hang of it. Certainly there is something very pleasing about cooking a large whole fish in a utensil designed especially for that purpose, but I find it overcooks the fish which I like just done and still firm and moist.

If you cook it in the oven, do be sure that the fish will actually fit in. On more than one occasion Tom and I have come home with a fish that was too big, even if put in diagonally. When that happens I cut off its head, cook the head separately (and lightly, to keep it intact), put the two together on my serving platter and hide the join with a garland of herbs or necklace of cucumber rings. Indeed, a fish's headlessness was a virtue on one occasion. We were entertaining someone who liked fish but could not bear to see a head staring at him from the plate. It was a fine looking fish we had that night. I took its head off to make soup for another day, cut a head-shaped slice of bread, toasted it, spread it with smoked salmon pâté, made an olive eye, a cucumber mouth and a collar of parsley, and our guest was quite happy.

If you are serving the fish warm, use butter in the preparation; if cold, use olive oil. Tarragon is excellent with salmon. Coriander is good too, as is basil or other leafy herbs. Not so good are the harder pungent ones, like sage or rosemary.

3 lb / 1½ kg salmon trout, scaled and gutted by your fishmonger
Salt, pepper, lemon juice

1 oz / 25 g butter or 1 tablespoon olive oil
Fresh herbs

Wipe the fish with a damp cloth to remove any traces of blood and scales. Oil or butter a piece of tinfoil large enough to completely enclose the fish. Place it on the foil. Salt and pepper the inside, just a pinch of each, and squeeze over it the juice of half a lemon. Seal the fish in the foil and bake in a pre-heated oven gas mark 3, 170°C/ 325°F, for 40–45 minutes. Remove and let it cool in the foil. When cool enough to handle, skin the fish carefully and lay on a flat serving dish. It is now yours to garnish as you wish. Bunches of fresh herbs surrounding it? Lovage leaves? Rose geranium leaves? Keep the cucumber and tomato slices for your salads. Serve summer sauce or mayonnaise with it.

A summer sauce

This very simple sauce is delicious served with warm, freshly cooked asparagus, new potatoes or River Tay salmon trout, or all three, since you are quite likely to have the same things at one meal (though that would be rather a surfeit of sauce). It also makes a fine dip for *crudités*, or a spread on fresh bread for sandwiches in place of butter. The quantities can be doubled, trebled or quadrupled. This is enough to serve four people with asparagus.

2 tablespoons thick plain yoghurt
2 tablespoons thick cream
2 or 3 cloves of the freshest garlic crushed with salt

6 tablespoons finely chopped fresh herbs – one or two or all of the following, depending on what you have available: parsley, basil, french tarragon, chives, watercress
Salt and pepper to taste

Mix all the ingredients, season to taste and spoon over asparagus, salmon trout or what you will.

Summer pudding
SERVES 4–6

I am never sure if strawberries are right in a summer pudding but have included them because they are so readily available.

Slices of crustless bread
1–2 oz / 25–50 g sugar
Some or all of the following to about 1½ lb / 700 g weight:
Raspberries
Loganberries

Redcurrants
Blackcurrants
Whitecurrants
Strawberries

Rinse and drain the fruit. Put in a pan and sprinkle the sugar over it. Set on a low heat until the juices run and the sugar melts. Add up to four tablespoons of water to encourage the juice. Check for sweetness. Remove from heat. Start lining the pudding basin. I find this works best if you cut square slices into two wedge-shaped pieces and place these narrow edge down in the basin. Continue, overlapping the slices slightly until the basin is fully lined. Cut a small circle to fit the bottom. Pour in the fruit to fill the basin. The bread will quickly absorb the juice, but reserve a few tablespoons of it. Fit slices of bread over the top so the fruit is completely covered. Cover with a saucer and place a weight on top to pack the whole thing as tightly as possible. Refrigerate. To serve unmould on to a plate and surround with the reserved juice. Serve cream or *crème fraîche* or ricotta or *fromage blanc* if you like.

A fancy way of preparing this is to cook all the fruit separately and arrange it in layers in the lined pudding basin with a layer of bread separating each. Mine has never really lasted long enough for this to be an important consideration.

TOMATO SOUP
GRILLED MONKFISH WITH BUTTERED RICE
GREEN SALAD
STRAWBERRIES IN RED WINE

Another useful menu in that some preparation can be done in advance, such as the soup and the marinading.

When I first started buying monkfish seven or eight years ago, I see from the records in my food diaries that it was then considerably cheaper than cod. Alas, this is no longer the case. In price it compares with the more expensive fish and certainly in France it is as highly regarded as sole. I cook monkfish often because it lends itself to many methods of preparation, some more usually associated with meat cookery. Here it is cooked rather after the fashion of a leg of lamb.

A soft, perfumy red wine such as a Bourgueil or Chinon would be excellent for the strawberries. I would be inclined to serve it with the fish too, perhaps lightly chilled. Monkfish cooked in the oven with herbs takes very kindly to a red wine. If not one of the Loire reds, then I would treat myself (and my strawberries) to a soft young red Graves from a *petit château* with this meal. We have much enjoyed a 1979 Château Crabitey of late.

This is really a tomato and vegetable soup. Tomato dominates, but the other ingredients give it a little extra body and flavour.

1 onion
1 carrot
1 stick of celery
1 lb / 450 g ripe tomatoes
2 whole cloves of garlic
1 tablespoon of olive or
    sunflower oil

½ pint / 300 ml stock
Salt, pepper and sugar to taste
Fresh basil, parsley or chives
Cream or yoghurt – optional

Heat the oil in a saucepan. Soften the chopped onion, carrot and celery in it for a few minutes. A little browning will not hurt, but the vegetables should not burn or your soup will be left with a bitter flavour.

When the other vegetables are soft, add the whole garlic cloves (which you needn't bother to peel since all bits will be sieved out) and the tomatoes roughly chopped but retaining skin, seeds and green stalks which all add to the flavour. Add the stock. Simmer until the carrots are soft, by which time everything else will be cooked. Cool a little, then purée and sieve. Season to taste. Serve sprinkled with fresh herbs, and a spoonful of cream or yoghurt if liked. I tend to serve tomato soup hot, but have also had it cold. It is good either way.

This dish can also be cooked in the oven like a roast.

If at all possible use fresh herbs; rosemary, thyme and sage are usually available, but I would go easy on the sage which can be overpowering. A mixture of your chosen herbs should also include some parsley.

2–2½ lb / 1 kg piece of
    monkfish
4 tablespoons olive oil
4 cloves garlic, crushed
Salt
Pepper

¼ pint / 150 ml white wine
2 shallots or one small mild
    onion, finely chopped
Herbs
3 tomatoes, peeled, seeded and
    roughly chopped

Remove all the skin from the monkfish. Even if it has been skinned by the fishmonger you will still need to remove the transparent skin and 'gristle' which would cause the fish to shrink during cooking if left on.

Marinate the fish for up to 24 hours before you need it, in the oil, wine, garlic, seasoning, herbs and onions. Pre-heat the grill, or the oven to gas mark 6, 200°C/400°F.

Drain the fish, leaving on the bits of herbs and garlic sticking to it, and reserve the marinade in a saucepan. Place on the grill rack or in a roasting tin and grill or bake for 20 minutes. Remove from the direct heat, but keep in a warm place while you make the sauce.

Take the marinade and reduce over fairly high heat, adding the chopped tomatoes. Cook for a further two to three minutes.

Serve the fish whole on a long serving dish, surrounded with the sauce and garnished with perhaps a few black olives and some more parsley. I feel that a dish of buttered rice would accompany this very well.

Green salad   I would serve a good salad with or after the fish, with plenty of different sorts of greens, and dress it with walnut oil and a touch of lime juice. Thus it becomes a dish in itself rather than an afterthought.

Some or all of the following greens and salad herbs:

Little Wonder lettuce	Coriander, purslane, flat
Mâche or corn salad	parsley
Watercress	Walnut oil
Rocket	A few crushed walnuts
Young dandelion leaves	Teaspoon of lime juice
Young nettle shoots	Sea salt
Oak leaf lettuce	Black pepper
Celery tops	

Stir the oil, lime juice, salt and pepper together in the bottom of a salad bowl. Add a pinch of mustard if you like. Cross the salad servers and pile on top your selection of washed or wiped and dried salad things. When ready to serve, turn in the dressing and scatter with herbs and crushed walnuts.

Strawberries in   This is so simple that it scarcely warrants a recipe. It is far more
red wine   interesting than strawberries and cream which is not to me a felicitous combination. Raspberries and cream, certainly, but strawberries and wine, please.

Wash or wipe and dry the best, ripest, but firm strawberries you can find. Slice the larger ones. Put into a white china basin or individual serving dishes. Sprinkle a fair amount of good red wine over them and let them macerate for up to an hour. Serve cold but not icily chilled.

POACHED EGGS WITH ARTICHOKES
TAGLIATELLE WITH WALNUT SAUCE
GREEN SALAD
HOT PEACHES AND CREAM

A good simple supper or lunch menu. Simple, that is, provided you have your artichoke bottoms readily available. You can of course buy tinned ones, but these are not nearly as good as the ones you prepare yourself. However, I have recently seen frozen ones, under the Bonduelle label, imported from Brittany. They seem to be just the right size for this sort of dish. With no meat or fish in the meal, it makes a suitable menu for vegetarians.

A light, white burgundy, such as a Montagny, is the kind of wine we serve with this. It is first mentioned in my food diaries at 80p a bottle!

4 large artichokes	½ pint / 300 ml stock (meat or vegetable)	*Poached eggs with artichokes*
1 oz / 25 g butter or margarine		
1 medium-sized onion, sliced	Salt, pepper to taste	SERVES 4
1 large bunch watercress	Tablespoon double cream	
	4 eggs	

The artichokes: Bring a large pan of water to the boil. Remove the stalk and outer leaves of the artichoke. Drop the artichokes in the pan and boil until tender – when a leaf comes away quite easily. Drain and cool. Remove all the leaves. Unless you are prepared to scrape off the flesh from the base of each leaf and save it for an omelette filling, then you do, I am afraid, have quite a lot of waste in this recipe. You could I suppose serve artichokes vinaigrette the day before you prepare this dish but make everyone promise to leave the base. Difficult because this is the best part. Remove the hairy choke by pulling it away a tuft at a time, or cutting it away with a sharp knife or teaspoon. I find this difficult to do and it removes too much of the flesh if I am not careful. Set aside and prepare the purée.

Watercress purée: Soften the onion in half the butter heated in a saucepan. Add the watercress and the stock. Bring to the boil and cook quite fiercely for a minute or two. This will be enough to soften the cress but not enough to dull its bright colour. Cool, blend and sieve. Pour back into the saucepan.

Eggs: Meanwhile poach the eggs for 3 minutes. Trim and keep warm in a basin full of warm water.

For the final preparation gently cook the artichoke bottoms in the remaining butter, more to warm them through rather than cook them any more. Place one in each heated, individual serving dish. Drain and dry the eggs and place on each artichoke heart. Heat up the purée and add the cream which will liaise with it. When hot, pour a spoonful on each egg and the rest on the side of the dish. Serve immediately.

Tagliatelle with walnut sauce
SERVES 4 AS A
MAIN COURSE,
6 AS A
STARTER

1 lb / 450 g tagliatelle, fresh, dried or homemade (see p. 25)
2 oz / 50 g butter
2 tablespoons olive oil
1 clove garlic, crushed

3 oz / 75 g freshly grated Parmesan, or a mixture of Parmesan and Pecorino
4 oz / 100 g walnut halves which you crush or grind yourself

Prepare the quickly made sauce by melting the oil and butter in a small heavy saucepan. Add the garlic and walnuts and cook for a minute or two. Add two-thirds of the cheese and let it melt into the sauce.

Cook and drain the pasta. Pour into an oiled serving dish and toss in the sauce. Sprinkle the rest of the cheese on top and serve immediately.

With this, or to follow it, a crisp green salad.

Hot peaches and cream
SERVES 4

Rich, easy and delicious.

4 ripe peaches
3 oz / 75 g sugar

½ pint / 300 ml double cream

Slice the peaches into an ovenproof dish – a white china flan dish, or individual flat dishes. Pour on the double cream and put under a medium grill to heat through. Turn the grill to high, remove the dish and sprinkle the sugar on evenly. Put it back under the grill and let it caramelise without catching. Serve while hot.

CRAB SALAD
RABBIT WITH HERBS
BROWN RICE
RASPBERRIES AND RICOTTA

Crabs are at their best in the summer. If you give your fishmonger a few days' notice, he or she will not only have picked you out the best one available but will perhaps clean it and dress it for you. If you prefer to do it yourself then have the fishmonger remove the (few) inedible parts.

Rabbit is a somewhat neglected meat here, which seems a pity as it is so tasty and lean. Much cooked in countries around the Mediterranean with the herbs which grow wild on the hillsides, rabbit lends itself well to a simple preparation.

I think if I couldn't find the best raspberries, I'd serve the ripest Cavaillon melons, chosen for their smell – if they smell melony they are ripe.

As I write this, the meal takes on more and more of a Mediterranean flavour and I think I might want to serve a cold ratatouille for starters rather than the crab salad which sounds so English.

With this very definitely southern meal we would probably serve wine from the appropriate region. A roughish white Châteauneuf-du-Pape rather than our fine 1982 Condrieu. A sparkling Clairette de Die would start this off as a dinner party. And nothing would finish it better than a glass of 1983 Muscat de Beaumes de Venise from Paul Jaboulet. It might almost grow next door to the melons.

Crab salad
SERVES 4

Your fishmonger will help you choose a crab which is heavy for its size. The meat contained in the claws is succulent and juicy, so choose one with large claws.

1 large, heavy crab	Lemon juice
2 oz / 50 g softened butter	Chives
½ pint / 300 ml homemade mayonnaise (see p. 82)	Salt and pepper
	6 slices brown bread

First remove the soft brown 'meat' from the shell of the crab. Sprinkle with a few drops of lemon juice and mix until smooth with the softened butter. Crack the claws and remove all the flesh. Fold it into the mayonnaise, add more lemon juice and finely chopped chives, and salt and pepper to taste.

Serve a portion of crab on each individual plate, garnished as much or as little as you like. Serve each with triangles of brown toast spread with the buttered crab.

Rabbit
with herbs
SERVES 4

For this dish use the back and hindquarters of a wild rabbit for a gamier taste, and tame rabbit for something a little more tender, but perhaps not quite so tasty. Use the forequarters for stock or minced up with other ingredients for a terrine. Start the dish the day before required. Use whatever herbs are fresh and available – thyme, marjoram, myrtle, parsley, basil etc.

3–3½ lb / 1.5 kg rabbit pieces on the bone	Tablespoon chopped fennel, if available
½ pint / 300 ml white wine	Fresh herbs
2 cloves garlic	Seasoned flour
1 onion, sliced	2 tablespoons fruity olive oil
1 carrot, sliced	Salt and pepper to taste
1 stick of celery, sliced	

Trim any fat and gristle away from the rabbit joints. Lay in a single layer in a china or earthenware dish. Pour over the wine. Add the vegetables (except the fennel) and some of the herbs. Marinate overnight.

The cooking time depends on whether you are using tame or wild rabbit, so you will need to take this into account when you start the final preparation. Drain and dry the rabbit, reserving the marinade. Heat a heavy iron frying pan or casserole. Ideally of course you should use a *sauteuse* but those receptacles already mentioned will do almost as well. Shake the rabbit joints in a paper bag with the seasoned flour. This will give them the required light coating if you blow off any excess. When the pan is hot, add the olive oil. Once this is smoking, place the rabbit joints in the pan in a single layer. Brown all over. Lower the heat. Moisten with a little of the strained marinade, add the fennel and the rest of the herbs and cook very gently. You will need to add more marinade from time to time to stop the pan from drying. When the meat is tender (about 40 minutes for tame rabbit, 1–1¼ hours for wild rabbit) taste for seasoning. Arrange the pieces on a suitable serving dish and garnish with bunches of fresh herbs.

Brown rice
SERVES 4

This takes longer to cook than white rice so start preparing it at the same time as the rabbit. Sometimes I dress it up with a few slivers of dried apricots, raisins and flaked almonds.

8 oz / 225 g long grain brown   Water
  rice   Pinch of salt
1 tablespoon olive oil

Heat the oil in a casserole. Stir in the rice until each grain is shiny and coated. Pour on twice the volume of water, add a pinch of salt. Bring to the boil and then turn down to the lowest possible heat. Cover the pan and let the rice cook very slowly. When all the liquid is absorbed, the rice is ready.

Raspberries and ricotta

Again, something simple that requires no recipe. You need the freshest ricotta and the ripest, freshest raspberries. Pick over the latter. They should be so good and their pedigree so impeccable that you will not need to wash them. Serve a small wedge of ricotta on each plate and scatter a few raspberries around it. Gluttons also serve cream poured over the ricotta.

FRESH PEA SOUP
GRILLED DUCK BREASTS
TOMATO AND BASIL SALAD
APRICOT SORBET

This is a versatile meal, suitable for a quickly prepared dinner party, particularly if you have at least a day's notice and can do some of the preparations in advance. But equally, as it uses very seasonal ingredients it's not expensive, and thus you may feel inclined to prepare it for a family, weekday meal. With some advance preparation it is the sort of menu you can put together in little more than half an hour at the end of a busy day. An added bonus is that, without looking at all spartan, it is relatively low in calories. The duck breast is grilled rather than fried, the courgettes are steamed, the sorbet uses natural fruit juice with no extra sugar, and the soup contains little or no cream, as you wish.

If I were serving this meal for a dinner party I would give my guests an excellent German wine. Some find it too sweet to accompany food but the wine is, to my palate, complex rather than sweet. The fragrance of the bouquet goes so well with fresh summer foods that I would not want to deprive my guests of that sensation of having wine and food which perfectly complement each other. And yes, I would go for one of the great '76s of which we have a few bottles left. Yes, it would be a Spätlese at least.

For a less grand occasion I would serve an English wine born in a good summer. There are few '76 English wines left now so I would serve a 1982, or preferably a 1983 Magdalen Rivaner from Diss in Norfolk. Or should I save that for another summer meal of Norfolk crab and samphire and instead serve an Elmham Park or Adgestone wine? 1984 was a good year for English wine.

Fresh pea soup
SERVES 4

Garden peas are available now, and for this soup you simply use the pods (as fresh as possible), keeping the peas for another dish. One of the most successful versions I made was from the last of the imported mangetouts, really quite coarse by the end of June; beside them, on the shelves, were the first of the English mangetouts, about a quarter of their size, so I used the large mangetouts for the soup and the small ones for garnish.

1 tablespoon sunflower oil
1 chopped onion
8 oz / 225 g mangetouts or empty pea pods
1 clove garlic – optional
1 pint / 600 ml stock
Herbs – 1 tablespoon of basil, tarragon, chervil or parsley

Seasoning to taste
Garnish – fresh peas, a sprig of herbs or tiny mangetouts, lightly steamed
1 spoonful of cream or yoghurt for each bowl

Heat the oil in a saucepan. Cook the chopped onion in it until soft. Break up the mangetouts or pea pods and stir in with the onions and garlic. Sprinkle with the merest hint of flour if you wish to absorb any remaining oil. Add the stock, bring to the boil and simmer until the mangetouts are tender. Add the herbs, stir into the soup, turn off the heat and cover with a lid to let the herbs perfume the liquid. When cooler, put through the blender and sieve. Serve hot or chilled depending on the weather and your mood, suitably garnished.

Grilled duck breasts
SERVES 4

Prepare these the day before required. The final cooking and serving will take 10 minutes at the most. You need four duck breasts. There is a variety of ways of obtaining these. The easiest is to buy two ducks and remove the breasts carefully. The beauty of this is that rather than being an extravagance the rest of the ducks provide you with meat for rillettes (p. 50), skin to crisp and serve instead of crispy bacon with fashionably hot salads, fat to render and save to cook potatoes in, thighs and drumsticks to preserve in a *confit* or to make a duck and olive casserole for a warming supper dish, carcasses for well flavoured stock, delicious giblets for soup and splendid livers for a pâté to serve on their own, with grapes and sautéed potatoes, or as a warm duck liver salad. To my mind this is by far the best way to buy duck breasts provided you have time to deal with the rest. If not, some butchers import the French *magret de canard*. These are very expensive, but large enough for two to serve four people. Now, too, the poultry counters of supermarkets sell quartered ducks. This is quite a good way of buying it because at least each piece gives you a portion of carcass with which to make the stock required for this recipe.

4 duck breasts	Pinch of fresh thyme
¼ pint / 150 ml dry white wine, white port or dry vermouth	½ pint / 300 ml unsalted duck stock
1 carrot	Parsley or chervil
1 onion	Seasoning to taste
1 stick of celery	Fruit jelly
2 cloves garlic	

Trim any fat and membranes from the duck breasts. Lay in a single layer in a dish. Spread the chopped vegetables over them and add the wine and the pinch of thyme. Cover and leave in the fridge overnight. When ready to cook, heat the grill-pan and rack very thoroughly. Remove the meat from the marinade, and wipe dry. Place the breasts flat on the rack. The meat will sizzle and have charred grill marks on it. This is intentional. Turn the grill lower after a minute and cook for a further 2–3 minutes depending on the thickness of the fillets and how rare or well done you like your meat. Remove the fillets and turn the heat up; once more the grill rack will be red hot and will mark the meat when you turn it over to grill the other side. After a minute or so, lower the heat and cook for a few more minutes. Remove and keep the fillets warm on a plate but away from any direct heat that would cook them further.

Meanwhile prepare the sauce. You will only serve a couple of spoonfuls of this which will be little more than a rich meat glaze. I like to cook sauces like this in a frying pan as the width allows the liquid to evaporate and reduce rapidly. Heat the pan and add the stock and the strained marinade. Simply let it reduce until you have a rich, syrupy sauce. Resist the temptation to add cream or butter. Only when it is ready to serve, taste it for seasoning and add as appropriate. If you made the mistake of salting the stock at any stage, the sauce will be inedibly salty. There is nothing you can do to salvage it, and you will have to serve the grilled duck with a pat of flavoured butter and pretend that you'd never intended to have a sauce with it.

To serve, you may like to leave the grilled fillets whole, or slice them partly through and fan out the slices on warmed individual serving plates. Add a spoonful or two of the sauce, a little fruit jelly, perhaps quince or gooseberry, and garnish with parsley or chervil and crisply steamed sticks or slices of courgettes.

To follow, rather than accompany this, I would serve a tomato salad – homegrown tomatoes are now available. The freshest and tastiest will need very little dressing. At this time of the year I don't bother to peel and deseed them as I enjoy every bit. Slice them thinly, salt very lightly, trickle on a little of your best olive oil and a grind or two of black pepper. Tomatoes have their own acidity so no lemon juice or vinegar is needed and if the tomatoes really are freshly picked and local, no pinch of sugar will be needed to bring out the flavour. To serve, roughly tear up some basil leaves and scatter these over the tomatoes. Olives, tarragon, parsley or coriander could all substitute.

Apricot sorbet
SERVES 4–6

After only a few summer weeks my *sorbetière* paid for itself. Not one of those new power-guzzling models but an updated Italian version of the old-fashioned ice-cream churn. Mine is electrical but still requires ice and salt. Some of my creations have been more successful than others. Regrettably those that had the best texture were also those that relied on a traditional sugar syrup. Not good for teeth, skin, heart or waistlines although delicious.

More recently, I have experimented with other types of mixture and I think the following recipe, which uses fresh juice and a little gelatine and glycerine, has a very acceptable texture. It is a recipe which you can use for almost any fruit. Some, like raspberries, strawberries and other soft fruits, you will use raw, others you may wish to poach. Try it too with some of the less common fruits – it makes them go a little further and thus it is relatively economical to make a sorbet from mango, papaya or guavas.

1 lb / 450 g apricots
1 pint / 600 ml unsweetened
  fruit juice – see method

4 sheets gelatine
1 dessertspoon glycerine

Because it is so rare to find perfectly ripe, golden apricots I find it is better to poach them a little first which allows the flavour to develop without destroying the real apricot flavour. For the fruit juice I use the kind you can now buy in cartons. The most suitable seem to be the apple juice which is best with sweeter fruit, and grape juice, with more natural sugar, which is best with fruit having more tartness.

Wash and stone the apricots. Place in a pan with half the juice. Poach until just soft – no more than four or five minutes.

Meanwhile soften the gelatine in the remaining juice. Strain the warm juice from the apricots on to the cold juice and gelatine which should then dissolve completely. Add the glycerine. Put the fruit and liquid into the blender and process until smooth. It is not necessary to sieve it. Let cool completely. Pour into the *sorbetière* and freeze. If you have no *sorbetière* or ice-cream maker, pour it into a tray and freeze in the ice-making compartment of the fridge, or in the freezer. You will need to stir it several times during freezing to stop ice crystals from forming. Serve neatly shaped oval portions on pretty small plates. Crystallised mint leaves garnish it well, as would a spoonful of apricot *coulis* made from rubbing extra cooked apricots through a sieve.

LE GRAND AÏOLI
GRILLED GOAT'S CHEESE ON TOAST
FRUIT TART

This is a fine, flexible meal, good to eat outdoors. You can add and subtract ingredients *selon le marché* and according to how many guests you have. The main ingredients are a strong, garlicky mayonnaise, a good piece of fish, some cooked potatoes, hard boiled eggs and olives, and then let your imagination take over. I like to serve quartered artichokes and broad beans with an aïoli and perhaps crab and some other shellfish.

Not a serious meal, but something to lounge over in the garden pretending you are in Provence, so I serve a slightly un-serious wine. Un-serious for us, that is, who hardly ever drink *rosé*. But on this occasion I would serve bottles of chilled, crisp, dry Tavel. If it was a small select dinner, something from the Domaine Ott, if I could find it.

A glass of Beaumes de Venise, well-chilled, would go very well with the tart.

Le grand aïoli
SERVES 6–8

Vegetables
Some or all of the following:

Carrots	Mangetout or garden peas
Green beans	Small artichokes
Celery	Olives
Cauliflower florets	Cherry tomatoes or the
Broccoli florets	smallest ordinary tomatoes
Spring onions	Lettuce hearts
Radishes	Small potatoes

Prepare the vegetables as appropriate. The potatoes and artichokes should be boiled or steamed until tender and allowed to cool. Green beans, peas, cauliflower and broccoli you will want to steam for just a very few minutes, so that they retain their colour and crispness. The rest of the vegetables would be nice served raw so that you get a variety of texture. Arrange the vegetables either on one large serving tray, or a few on each individual plate leaving enough room for the fish and the aïoli.

Fish

The traditional fish for this is salt cod which you soak for hours before simmering. If you cannot get it, fresh fish is fine. Ask your fishmonger to cut it from the thickest piece, and to skin it for you.

1½–2 lb / 600–900 g cod or   1 tablespoon olive oil
  haddock fillet   Salt and pepper to taste

Oil a piece of foil or greaseproof paper. Salt and pepper the fish and seal it in the foil or greaseproof paper. Put the parcel on a baking tray and cook in a pre-heated oven for 15–20 minutes at gas mark 5–6, 190–200°C / 375–400°F. Remove and let it cool in its parcel. This way all the flavour and juices are retained. Arrange the fish with the vegetables, not flaked, but in fairly large chunks.

Aïoli

There are different versions of this. Some insist on soft white breadcrumbs; I generally make a simple, very garlicky mayonnaise. If you have brought home gallons of olive oil from your holiday, then by all means use it. I begrudge this slightly and generally use two-thirds sunflower oil to one-third olive oil.

4 cloves garlic   Lemon juice or vinegar
2 egg yolks   Salt and pepper to taste
½ pint / 300 ml good oil

Crush the garlic cloves. Mix with the egg yolks and add the oil a drop at a time, beating or stirring continuously. Once the oil and egg emulsify (start to combine and thicken) you can add the oil in a thin stream, but beat all the while otherwise it might curdle. When all the oil is used up, flavour with a few drops of lemon juice or vinegar, and season to taste. You should end up with a very thick mayonnaise. Serve with the fish and vegetables as a dip.

Grilled goat's cheese on toast See page 58 for recipe.

Fruit tart

This is once again the sort of dish that allows you to use your imagination and needs no prescriptive recipe.

For the base, bake a shortbread, shortcrust or sponge case. Allow it to cool. Cover with a layer of filling – whipped cream, thick yoghurt, *crème patissière* or *crème fraîche*. Then arrange in concentric circles or wedges a display of perfect prepared fruits (cooked if necessary), providing plenty of contrasting colour; strawberries, blueberries, nectarines, dark plums, greengages for example. Then glaze with a thinned-down redcurrant or other fruit jelly, or make up a fresh fruit juice and gelatine mix for a firmer glaze.

JELLIES AND PRESERVES

I have never had a big country kitchen but the instinct is there nevertheless. I want to take some of those delicious summer flavours with me through into the autumn and winter, so in August and September out come the big pans, the scales, the preserving jars, the wine vinegar and the spices.

Because space in my cupboards is limited, I think carefully about what is going to be most useful, most appreciated during the coming months. We eat little jam ourselves, but remembering how popular edible presents are, I always make a few small jars to give away at Christmas; greengage, damson, cherry, apricot, with decorative labels and print fabric caps.

The soft fruits I tend to use for the clear, bright jellies which I like to serve with game and other meat dishes. Redcurrant is the traditional one, but there are so many other possibilities – gooseberry, elderberry and wild bramble, blackcurrant and cranberry. And even more unusual combinations, pear and cranberry, crabapple and rosemary. Blueberries are expensive but a small quantity of blueberry jelly is a luxury standby for lazy breakfasts. I once found some Chinese pears in the supermarket which tasted of pears and smelled of quinces. Not knowing quite when and how to fit them into a meal, I made a fragrant gold jelly from them which I used to serve with wild duck. Quince jelly is perhaps my favourite and I will sometimes make it go further by adding Bramley apples at the first stage. Apple jelly with different herbs added is also good with meat. The most unusual jelly has been my rhubarb and lavender jelly.

2 lb / 900 g rhubarb (prepared weight)
Water to cover
Bunch of lavender in bud (about 20 stems)

Juice of two lemons
Sugar

Rhubarb and lavender jelly

Wash the rhubarb. Cut into chunks and put in a pan. Simmer in $1-1\frac{1}{2}$ pints / 600–900 ml water until tender, together with half of the lavender buds removed from the stems. Strain through muslin or a jelly bag, without forcing, otherwise the jelly will be cloudy. Measure the liquid and add 1 lb / 450 g sugar for each pint / 600 ml of liquid. Squeeze the lemons, strain the juice and add to the liquid together with all but a few of the lavender buds wrapped in muslin. Bring to the boil and boil fast for 10 minutes or so until setting point is reached. Remove the lavender flowers and pour into heated jars. Add one sprig of lavender to each jar of jelly; seal and label.

This makes an exotic gift, goes well with meat dishes, but is delicious on hot toast or scones.

I make all my jellies up in the same basic way.

Fruits preserved in liqueur make excellent presents and are a good pudding standby. I buy *eau-de-vie* for this in France, or use an inexpensive vodka. Greengages and mirabelles, the small golden plums, keep well, as do kumquats, the tiny oval orange-like fruit, either sliced or whole.

If you have the patience and can remember what stage you have reached, a rum pot is a good thing to start early in the summer. If you keep it well stocked it will be ready to broach at Christmas. Starting with strawberries, add layers of fruit (not citrus fruits) as they come into season, covering each layer with rum.

Pickles do not appeal to me to the same extent but there are three things that I like to prepare at the end of the summer — garden cucumbers made into sweet pickle, tiny onions in wine or cider vinegar, and pickled samphire for serving with raw fish or fish salads throughout the autumn and winter.

For all these I only use wine or cider vinegar, not malt vinegar which I find too strong, and certainly not that horror of horrors, non-brewed condiment. None of the vegetables are cooked first but they do need to be prepared. The cucumbers are sliced, quite thickly, layered with salt and left overnight to disgorge their liquid. They are then well rinsed, dried and packed into clean kilner jars.

The pickled onions are peeled and prepared in salt the same way, then washed, dried and packed into jars. I find that samphire does not require this treatment as it is (a) salty enough and (b) does not tend to give off excess liquid and thus dilute the vinegar. Just wash, dry and pack into jars.

I like to use a sweetish spiced vinegar with cider vinegar or white wine vinegar as the base.

1 quart / 1.2 l vinegar	1 stick of cinnamon	*Spiced vinegar*
Teaspoon each of whole allspice and cloves	1 small piece of fresh ginger 1 lb / 450 g sugar	

Put the vinegar, spices and sugar in a narrow earthenware jug or jar and heat it in a pan of water. When the water boils, remove the pan from the heat and let the vinegar steep for a couple of hours. Strain it and pour over the prepared vegetables in the jar.

Seal, label and date. You should keep at least a month in a cool dry place before using.

Another jar of goodies to serve at Christmas is prunes in tea and brandy. Pack good plump prunes into a preserving jar. Half-fill with freshly made hot, strong tea and top up with brandy. Seal. Shake once or twice. Leave undisturbed until Christmas.

MAIN INDEX

INDEX OF WINES, SPIRITS, LIQUEURS, ETC.